Napoleon's French Army

1796–1815

History, Organisation and Equipment

GABRIELE ESPOSITO

HISTORIC ARMIES SERIES, VOLUME 6

Front cover image: Line infantry voltigeurs on the march. (Photo: Voltigeurs of the 18th Line Regiment, © Jan Štábl)

Title page image: Private of the Artillery Train of the Imperial Guard. (Photo: Le Livre, l'Histoire et l'Obusier, © Rose-Hélène Ledanseur)

Contents page image: NCO of the cuirassiers. (Photo: 2ème Régiment de Dragons, © Pauline Wilmotte)

Back cover image: NCO of the line infantry voltigeurs. (Photo: Voltigeurs of the 18th Line Regiment, © Jan Štábl)

About the Author

Gabriele Esposito is a military historian who works as a freelance author and researcher for publishing houses in the military history sector. In particular, he is an expert specialising in uniformology. His interests and expertise range from ancient civilisations to modern post-colonial conflicts. During recent years, he has conducted research on the military history of non-European countries. His books and essays are published on a regular basis by international publishers. He is the author of numerous military history articles appearing in specialised magazines.

Acknowledgements

This book is dedicated to my beloved parents, Maria Rosaria and Benedetto. A very special mention goes to the brilliant re-enactment groups that collaborated with me and their photos appear in this title. Without the incredible research of their members, this publication would not be the same. I want to express my deep gratitude to the following living history associations: Association Jean Roch Coignet, Premier Bataillon du Premier Régiment de Grenadiers à Pied de la Garde Impériale; Le Livre, l'Histoire et l'Obusier; 2ème Régiment de Dragons; Les chasseurs à cheval de la Grande Armée – 12ème régiment; 33ème Regiment d'Infanterie de Ligne; Pascal Thonon; Voltigeurs of the 18th Line Regiment.

Published by Key Books
An imprint of Key Publishing Ltd
PO Box 100
Stamford
Lincs PE9 1XQ

www.keypublishing.com

The right of Gabriele Esposito to be identified as the author of this book has been asserted in accordance with the Copyright, Designs and Patents Act 1988 Sections 77 and 78.

Copyright © Gabriele Esposito, 2025

ISBN 978 1 80282 791 0

Typeset by SJmagic DESIGN SERVICES, India.

Contents

Introduction

Napoleon's *Grande Armée* was one of the most perfect military machines that the history of the world has ever seen. It consisted of many units, each of which had a specific role on the battlefield. I aim to present a detailed overview of the organisation, uniforms and weapons of the French Army during the Napoleonic period.

The foot regiments of the line and light infantry represented the most important components of the French Army during the Napoleonic period; they were much more numerous than the units of the other branches and comprised the bulk of the rank-and-file soldiers. The other corps of the *Grande Armée*, such as the cavalry or the artillery, were not fundamental from a quantitative point of view but from a qualitative one: their members were professionals with specific training and equipment to perform precise tactical roles on the battlefield.

The Emperor's infantrymen were not elite soldiers. The French common infantryman, however, was intelligent, aggressive, well-disciplined and extremely resilient: he had total trust in his commander and was strongly determined to export the ideals of the Revolution to the other countries of Europe with the point of his bayonet.

The French cavalry of the Napoleonic period was the strongest on the European continent, as Wellington confirmed on several occasions. Napoleon used to say that 'cavalry is useful before, during and after the battle'; this was particularly true for his own mounted regiments, of which there were three main tactical categories. The cavalry of the *Grande Armée* consisted of heavy, medium and light divisions; and each comprised two units – cuirassiers and carabiniers for the heavy cavalry, dragoons and lancers for the medium cavalry, and hussars and mounted chasseurs for the light cavalry.

Napoleon began his military career as an artillery officer and was always interested in the quality of that particular service, which he considered to be decisive for winning battles. The French artillery was the best in Europe prior to 1789, after being reformed by the brilliant Lieutenant General Gribeauval around 1765. It was equipped with excellent guns and was precisely trained, with technically competent professional officers. Napoleon was the first military commander to use artillery offensively, by assembling hundreds of field pieces in 'grand batteries' that could hammer the enemy in view of frontal infantry attacks.

The guns of the new Gribeauval System could move rapidly both on and off the roads. This new and increased mobility favoured the development of the horse artillery, which soon reached a standard of excellence in Napoleon's military forces. In addition to the foot artillery and horse artillery, the technical units of the *Grande Armée* comprised corps that rarely fought on the battlefield but whose contribution to the success of the army was fundamental.

The engineers were the most important of the technical corps, and provided highly specialised contingents of *sapeurs* or sappers, as well as a good number of competent officers who could perform a considerable variety of functions.

Chapter 1

Line Infantry

HISTORY AND ORGANISATION

Establishment of 1799

When Napoleon became the First Consul of the French Republic in 1799, he inherited a well organised and large line infantry. It consisted of 86 half or 'demi' brigades, each with three battalions. In the closing year of the 18th century, the French Republic comprised 96 administrative districts, so almost every district of France provided a demi-brigade of line infantry. These brigades were numbered in progressive order from 1 to 99, but there were several vacant numbers including 31, 38, 41, 49, 68, 71, 83, 87, 90, 91, 97, 98 and 99. Some of the administrative departments that made up the French Republic were not, in fact, French, but annexed by France in recent history. There were 18 of these in total and they were organised during the period 1792–98: two in Italy (Chambery and Nice, taken from Piedmont in 1792–93), two in Switzerland, one in southern France (the territory of Avignon, which had previously been part of the Papal States), nine in Belgium (France annexed the Austrian Netherlands in 1796), and four in Germany (these were located on the right bank of the Rhine and were taken from the Holy Roman Empire). However, despite these districts being acquired from vanquished foreign nations, their populations had a distinct French character and were easily absorbed into the French nation.

By the time of Napoleon's military coup, the designation *demi-brigade de bataille* (meaning half-brigade for battle) had already been replaced by *demi-brigade de ligne* (meaning half-brigade of the line) and a separation between line and light infantry had occurred. The First Consul did nothing to change the internal organisation of his line infantry units for some years.

- Each demi- or half-brigade, consisting of three battalions, had a homogenous composition in terms of training and experience.
- A single battalion consisted of one elite grenadier company and nine regular fusilier companies.
- A single regular company consisted of one captain, one lieutenant, one sub-lieutenant, one sergeant-major, five sergeants, one corporal-fourrier, eight corporals, two drummers and 104 privates.
- The elite grenadier companies had a similar structure, but with four sergeants and 64 privates.
- The staff of each half-brigade (meaning the senior officers commanding the whole half-brigade and not attached to any specific company) comprised one colonel, three battalion commanders, one adjutant, one paymaster, one drum-major, three standard-bearers, one surgeon, four assistant-surgeons, one shoemaker, one gaiter maker, one gunsmith, one tailor and eight musicians.

On 24 September 1803, Napoleon replaced the term demi-brigade with 'regiment'. The passage from half-brigade to regiment did not affect the numbering of the units or their internal structure. During that year, however, Napoleon had to restructure his line infantry when several regiments had to be raised again following the French defeat in Haiti. Haiti was the richest and most flourishing of France's colonies, but since the outbreak of the Revolution, a series of revolts by Haitian plantation slaves had gradually disrupted French authority. After becoming First Consul, Napoleon attempted to restore order in the Caribbean colony and sent a large expeditionary force there. While there, several

***Above left**: Aide-de-camp (staff officer) of the French Army, wearing campaign dress with shako.
(Photo: Le Livre, l'Histoire et l'Obusier, © Rose-Hélène Ledanseur)*

***Above middle**: Non-Commissioned Officer (NCO) of the Foot Grenadiers of the Imperial Guard.
(Photo: Association Jean Roch Coignet, Premier Bataillon du Premier Régiment de Grenadiers à Pied de la Garde
Impériale, © Jean-François Darius)*

***Above right**: NCO of the Foot Grenadiers of the Imperial Guard, wearing parade dress.
(Photo: Le Livre, l'Histoire et l'Obusier, © Rose-Hélène Ledanseur)*

demi-brigades de ligne were wiped out by yellow fever as well as revolutionary slaves (who were supported by Britain). As a result, Haiti became an independent republic. New regiments were raised including the 100th, 101st, 102nd, 103rd, 104th, 105th, 106th, 107th, 108th, 111th and 112th (numbers 109 and 110 remained vacant).

Changes in 1803 and 1804 and the Introduction of a Company of Voltigeurs

During 1803, the artillery company that was an addition to each active battalion was officially abolished. From there, Napoleon restructured his line infantry battalions, this time introducing a new category of elite soldiers known as *voltigeurs* (skirmishers). Their name literally translates as 'acrobats' and derives from the tactical duties they were expected to perform. According to his plan, each infantry battalion needed a number of skirmishers who could move in open formation in front of the fusilier companies that advanced in line or column formations. The light skirmishers were tasked with securing the terrain in front of their advancing comrades, and with engaging the enemy from a distance by accurately firing at them from covert positions. Scouting and skirmishing were difficult operations for which soldiers needed specific training and equipment. The new voltigeurs were to be the eyes and ears of the line battalions thanks to their superior mobility, which enabled them to advance rapidly on every kind of terrain.

By 1804, the French line infantry consisted of 97 regiments. Up until that point, the French army did not include *light* infantry companies in its *line* infantry battalions. At that time, 'chasseurs', translated as hunters and denoting light infantrymen, were a separate component of the French infantry and had their own autonomous demi-brigades/regiments.

In order to retain the standard number of ten companies for each battalion, Napoleon ordered the second company of fusiliers in each line infantry battalion to retrain its members as voltigeurs. This company would be an elite sub-unit, much like the grenadier company that headed up each battalion. With this reform, from 1804, each line infantry battalion had two elite companies (one grenadier and one voltigeur) and eight fusilier companies.

The creation of the voltigeurs, who were the light infantrymen of the line units, was not completely new, since previous auxiliary battalions included one company of chasseurs (the light infantrymen of the light units.

The new voltigeurs soon became skilled at sharpshooting, since they received specific training in marksmanship and learned how to fire from covert positions. Eventually, the voltigeur companies started to be detached – quite frequently – from their parent battalions in order to form temporary ad hoc battalions of elite skirmishers. These were employed to conduct special operations, such as storming enemy positions or conducting long-range scouting missions. When a line infantry battalion was deployed in line on the battlefield, the grenadier company was placed on the right and the voltigeur company on the left of its formation, flanking the centrally located fusiliers. Thanks to their superior mobility, the voltigeurs worked efficiently with the cavalry branch of the army, which could support mounted skirmishes with their accurate fire.

Generally, the grenadiers were chosen from the tallest and strongest recruits assigned to each battalion, while the voltigeurs were chosen from the smallest men, since they had to move very rapidly. In addition, both grenadiers and voltigeurs already had combat experience, since they were chosen from veterans with several years of service.

The general structure of the French line infantry saw no further significant changes until 1808. These were the years of Napoleon's greatest victories and of the proclamation of the Empire. The French line infantrymen showed all their valour in a series of memorable pitched battles at Ulm, Austerlitz, Jena, Auerstadt, Eylau and Friedland. The 1805 campaign against Austria, in particular, offers a perfect example of Napoleon's innovative employment of his line regiments. By moving faster than their enemies and by living off the land, the French infantrymen could travel enormous distances in just a few days, surprising their enemies with audacious outflanking manoeuvres that gave them precious superiority.

The French fusiliers were well disciplined and could adapt to any tactical situation; they had no fear of launching frontal bayonet assaults and knew how to fight in line by firing their muskets from a short distance. They were trained to make personal sacrifices and had incredible resistance, while their company officers were intelligent and audacious, earning their ranks on merit. The backbone of the regiments was represented by the veteran non-commissioned officers (NCOs), who offered an example to follow for the ranks.

Changes in 1808

On 18 February 1808, Napoleon partly modified the organisation of his line infantry, by enlarging it but without creating new regiments. Each line infantry regiment was now to consist of four active battalions (instead of three) – known as *bataillons de guerre* – plus one depot battalion; the latter was to be smaller than the others, and would consist of just four fusilier companies.

A single *bataillon de guerre* was to comprise one company of grenadiers, one company of voltigeurs and four companies of fusiliers (instead of eight). Overall, a line infantry regiment now had four companies of grenadiers, four companies of voltigeurs, 16 companies of fusiliers and four depot companies. The depot companies were mostly tasked with providing new recruits to the *bataillons de guerre*.

- The staff of each regiment was to consist of: one colonel, one major, four battalion commanders, five adjutants, five assistants, ten sergeant-majors, three standard-bearers, one drum-major, one drum-corporal, one band-master, seven musicians, four craftsmen, one quartermaster, one paymaster, one surgeon-major and four assistant-surgeons.
- A single company comprised one captain, one lieutenant, one sub-lieutenant, one sergeant-major, four sergeants, one corporal-quartermaster, eight corporals, two drummers and 121 privates. The grenadier and *voltigeur* companies also had this standard internal establishment.

NCO of the Foot Grenadiers of the Imperial Guard, wearing campaign dress. (Photo: Association Jean Roch Coignet, Premier Bataillon du Premier Régiment de Grenadiers à Pied de la Garde Impériale, © Jean-François Darius)

Grenadiers had to be chosen from soldiers with four years of service and who had participated in at least two of the following battles: Ulm, Austerlitz, Jena and Friedland. A grenadier had to be at least 173.5cm tall.

Voltigeurs had to be chosen from the soldiers who had two years of service; they could not be taller than 150cm. Both the grenadiers and the voltigeurs received higher pay than the fusiliers due to their elite status.

The depot battalion was commanded by a major who was never sent to the front in war. Each of its four companies had a different function: the 4th Company never left the depot and was mostly tasked with outfitting and training new recruits (for this reason it was assisted by a dressing captain and by a quartermaster-treasurer). Attached to the 4th Company were the so-called *enfants de troupe* – sons or orphans of soldiers who were on the battalion's payroll – and the veteran soldiers who were awaiting retirement or pensioning. The 1st Company and 3rd Company were responsible for transferring the newly trained recruits to the active battalions; the 2nd Company was generally employed to perform garrison duties in the various military facilities.

Special Ranks

The four *bataillons de guerre* of each regiment each included four *sapeurs,* or sappers, who were attached to the grenadier company and who were under the command of a pioneer corporal (there was one NCO for each regiment). The sappers were to act as combat engineers. Their main task was to build field fortifications as well as to remove any obstacle encountered by their battalion during the march. Formally, they had the same status and privileges as the grenadiers.

Musicians were a fundamental component of Napoleon's line infantry and a separate rank in each battalion, since they transmitted the orders of the officers to the ranks in the chaos of battle. Most of the line infantry musicians were young boys, orphans or sons of soldiers, who earned a living by being part of the army. Grenadier and fusilier companies had drummers, while voltigeur companies had cornets. The musicians of the regimental staff (a separate group) had a special status compared to the musicians of single companies; they symbolised the martial spirit and traditions of the regiment and marched at the head of it during parades. For these reasons, they wore extravagant uniforms, enjoyed a series of privileges and were commonly known as the 'head of the column'. The drum-major led all the musicians of a regiment: on most occasions he was a veteran of many campaigns and had a special relationship with his younger comrades. Often, he had the most ornate dress.

Standard-bearers were another fundamental component of the regimental staff; one of them, in particular, had the honour of carrying the Imperial Eagle of his regiment on the battlefield. The Imperial Eagle, like those of ancient Roman legions, was a symbol of the soldiers' loyalty towards their Emperor and thus was the most precious possession of each regiment. Losing it in battle was a tragedy, and could destroy the reputation of a regiment. The importance of an Imperial Eagle was so great that the other two standard-bearers of each regiment escorted the senior standard-bearer.

The internal organisation of the French line infantry units introduced in 1808 remained practically unchanged until the end of the Napoleonic Period in 1815. During the years 1808–15, however, the foot troops increased in number with the formation of many new battalions. Several of the existing regiments added a 5th, 6th or even 7th Battalion to their four *bataillons de guerre.*

New Regiments

Due to the territorial expansion of the Empire, Napoleon now had the resources to populate new regiments. The first of these was the 113th Regiment, established in May 1808. It was formed by converting an infantry regiment from Tuscany into a French line regiment unit. From 1801, the Grand Duchy of Tuscany, one of many Italian states, became a French puppet state known as the Kingdom of Etruria. Tuscany had a small army that comprised a single infantry regiment of good quality. In December 1807, Napoleon absorbed the Kingdom of Etruria into his Empire and so this unit became part of the French line infantry, known as the new 113th Regiment.

During 1807, in view of his impending invasion of Spain, Napoleon organised seven provisional regiments of line infantry from new recruits; following the conquest of the Iberian Peninsula in 1808, these were transformed into permanent units and were absorbed into the French line infantry (becoming the 114th, 115th, 116th, 117th, 118th, 119th and 120th Regiments).

The Reserve Legions

On 20 March 1807, in order to have some military reserves that could be employed to defend the frontiers of his Empire while he was away fighting, Napoleon ordered the creation of the so-called

Above left: Private of the Foot Grenadiers of the Imperial Guard, wearing winter great coat. (Photo: Association Jean Roch Coignet, Premier Bataillon du Premier Régiment de Grenadiers à Pied de la Garde Impériale, © Jean-François Darius)

Above middle: NCO of the Foot Grenadiers of the Imperial Guard, wearing service dress with bicorn. (Photo: Le Livre, l'Histoire et l'Obusier, © Rose-Hélène Ledanseur)

Above right: A sapper of the Foot Grenadiers of the Imperial Guard. (Photo: Association Jean Roch Coignet, Premier Bataillon du Premier Régiment de Grenadiers à Pied de la Garde Impériale, © Jean-François Darius)

légions de réserve de l'intérieur or reserve legions of the interior. There were five in total and their bases were in Lille, Metz, Rennes, Versailles and Grenoble. Each of the five legions consisted of four line infantry companies and were comparable to a battalion numerically. According to Napoleon's original plans, the reserve legions were not to operate outside France. However, three of them were sent to fight in Spain during the last months of 1807. As a result, in January 1809, the five *légions de réserve de l'intérieur* were absorbed into the regular line infantry and became the 121st Regiment (raised from the 1st and 2nd Reserve Legion) and 122nd Regiment (raised from the 3rd, 4th and 5th Reserve Legion).

The Former Dutch Regiments

In 1810, the Kingdom of Holland, which had been ruled as a puppet state of France since 1806 by Napoleon's brother Louis Bonaparte, was annexed to the Empire. Its armed forces were absorbed into the French Army and became the following new units during 1810: 123rd, 124th, 125th and 126th Regiments. The 126th Regiment was disbanded in 1813 and its members were absorbed into the 123rd.

In 1811, another two units were added to the French line infantry, by converting three corps of Honour Guards (ceremonial units) into regular units. The Honour Guards of Hamburg and Lübeck became the 127th Regiment, while the Honour Guards of Bremen became the 128th Regiment. In the same year, soldiers of the German states of Oldenburg and Westphalia that were partly annexed to France, became the new 129th Regiment.

Back in 1809, to increase the infantry units available to fight in Spain, Napoleon had formed seven temporary auxiliary battalions by assembling different detachments of line infantry regiments that were already serving in the Iberian Peninsula. In 1811, these battalions were assembled to form two new regular regiments (one of line infantry and one of light infantry). The 1st, 3rd and 6th Auxiliary Battalions became the 130th Line Regiment, while the 2nd, 4th, 5th and 7th Auxiliary Battalions became the 34th Light Regiment. The year 1811 saw the formation of three more line infantry regiments: the 131st, 132nd and 133rd. The first two were made up of French conscripts, while the third was obtained by converting an existing unit of Italian conscripts.

On 8 June 1808, following the annexation of Tuscany to the Empire, Napoleon ordered the organisation of a new battalion to be made up of conscripts coming from the new Italian departments, which had hitherto 'resisted' conscription. This semi-penal unit had a light infantry character from its foundation and became a regiment in 1810 (with five battalions). Its official denomination was 1st Mediterranean Regiment. In March 1811, a 2nd Mediterranean Regiment of the same kind was organised, but this was soon absorbed into the French line as the 133rd Regiment.

Continued Expansion

Despite the disastrous Russian campaign of 1812 in which Napoleon suffered enormous human losses, Napoleon continued to expand his line infantry by creating new regiments. In January 1813, the 134th Regiment was formed from the recently disbanded *Garde de Paris*, (*see* chapter 3, Special Infantry Units). During 1813, in order to face the Allies in Germany with a sufficient number of soldiers, the Emperor made use of the National Guard (a military auxiliary force) to increase the manpower at his disposal. As a result, several units of the National Guard, organised with cohorts of the same strength as the previous battalions, were assembled to form a number of line regiments. Each department of the Empire was to provide a cohort (battalion) of infantrymen to the National Guard and therefore thousands of men were at its disposal.

The following new regiments were created during 1813 by assembling cohorts of various districts: 135th, 136th, 137th, 138th, 139th, 140th, 141st, 142nd, 143rd, 144th, 145th, 146th, 147th, 148th, 149th, 150th, 151st, 152nd, 153rd, 154th, 155th and 156th. These new units were of poorer quality than those that existed prior to the Russian Campaign. In most cases, they consisted of national guardsmen or recruits who were too young to have any military experience. The French conscript of 1814 became known as 'Marie-Louise', a nod to his feminine appearance as he was too young to have a beard. The expression 'Marie-Louise' also came also from the fact that Napoleon's wife, Marie-Louise, issued the decrees of October 1813, ordering 280,000 new conscripts to be recruited. For the first time, conscription was

Fusiliers of the line infantry in 1805; the figure on the right has winter great coat.

extended to young people aged 18. The decrees promulgated by the Empress were a shock for most French families.

France was under the threat of a foreign invasion and thus every able-bodied man was required to defend the frontiers. The conscripts of 1813–14 received superficial training lasting just two weeks before they were sent to the front. Despite this, they fought with great courage to defend their homeland. In the French campaign of 1814, the Grande Armée lacked uniforms, equipment and weaponry. In addition, the infantry was unfamiliar with the harsh conditions typical of a winter campaign.

Following the abdication of Napoleon on 12 May 1814, the restored monarchy reduced the number of line infantry regiments. All the new units numbered 113 to 156, created during 1808–14, were disbanded, alongside a few others to reduce the tally of line infantry units to 90. With the adoption of this new structure, all the regimental numbers that had remained vacant thus far were brought into use, with line infantry units now numbered from 1 to 90.

When Napoleon returned to France in 1815 following exile, he retained the new structure of 90 line infantry regiments but restored the old numeration with vacant numbers. The old system that he reverted to was inherited from the revolutionary period so had a certain ideological significance. Generally, the reduction in units ordered by the restored monarchy in 1814 had positive implications, since the remaining units could fill their ranks with the best elements of the disbanded units. As a result, the line infantry regiments commanded by Napoleon at Waterloo in 1815 were of better quality that those of 1814.

UNIFORMS

In 1799, the French line infantry wore the 'national uniform' introduced in 1793. It featured a black bicorn with national cockade comprising an orange-yellow lace holder and red-over-white pompom made of wool. A dark blue long-tailed coat had brass buttons, white frontal lapels piped in red, dark blue shoulder straps piped in red, a red collar piped in white, red round cuffs piped in white, white cuff flaps piped in red, white turn-backs piped in red, and horizontal pocket flaps on the back of the coat piped in red and decorated with three buttons. Also included were a white waistcoat, white trousers, black gaiters during cold months or white gaiters during hot months, and black shoes. This was the standard dress of the fusiliers.

Grenadiers

The grenadiers wore a black bearskin with brass frontal plate bearing a flaming grenade; the bearskin had a decorative red crown on the back with a white cross, red plume on the left with a national cockade at its base, red decorative cords and flounders, black leather peak. They were each issued a dark blue long-tailed coat with brass buttons and white frontal lapels piped in red, red fringed epaulettes, a red collar piped with white, red rounded cuffs piped with white, white cuff flaps piped in red, and white turn-backs piped in red and featuring decorative red flaming grenades embroidered on them. Horizontal pocket flaps on the back of the coat were piped in red and decorated with three buttons. The outfit was complete with a white waistcoat, white trousers, black gaiters during cold months or white gaiters during hot months, and black shoes.

A few features of the uniform were modified over time: the tails of the coat became shorter to be more practical and the front lapels had an accentuated curve. According to official dress regulations, the collar and cuffs had to be red with white piping, but it was not uncommon to see white collar and cuffs with red piping; dark blue cuff flaps with red piping were also quite common and sometimes the cuff flaps were completely absent from the coat. These variations derived from the fact that uniforms were produced locally.

Other non-regulation modifications included the lack of red piping on the front lapels and the use of vertical pocket flaps on the back of the coat (instead of the horizontal ones prescribed by regulations). The decorative badges embroidered on the white turn-backs of the tails were regularly present on the uniforms of grenadiers. On most occasions, fusiliers did not have them or displayed a huge variety of different badges such as stars, eagles, diamonds or hearts. After 1804, eagle badges became the most popular.

The black bicorn hat, the standard headgear of the French line infantry, was worn on the head in two different positions according to the activities of its wearer: when worn across the head (*en bataille*) its wearer was ready to fight, and when worn fore-and-aft (*en colonne*), its wearer was marching. Pompoms gradually replaced the previous tufts made of wool and were usually half-red and half-white. Later, however, the colour of the pompom changed for each fusilier company and thus became a mark of distinction. Grenadiers wore their massive bearskins on campaign and on parade, but could use the standard bicorn on other occasions; sometimes the cords and flounders of the bearskin could be white instead of red.

Both the fusiliers and the grenadiers also used the *bonnet de police* undress cap: this was dark blue with red piping and had a tasselled stocking end folded up and tucked behind the right-hand side of a stiffened headband. The tassel was red and on the front of the cap there was a red flaming grenade for grenadier companies. When not used, the *bonnet de police* was rolled and strapped under the cartridge box of each soldier.

According to the egalitarian principles of the Revolution, officers were dressed exactly like their men, but their uniforms were made of finer material. The lace holder of the bicorn's cockade was golden for officers. In addition, they wore a gilt *gorget* under their neck. This was mostly used on parade and incorporated decorative silver devices that usually included unit number and – after

**Grenadier of the line infantry wearing bicorn.
(Photo: 33ème Regiment d'Infanterie de Ligne,
© Bartosz Janiczek)**

1804 – an Imperial Eagle. The gorget was the last remnant of the medieval knight's armour, a symbol of high military status.

Officers displayed their rank on their uniforms with epaulettes decorated with gold lace worn on the shoulders. These were designed according to a general scheme that had been introduced in 1786 and remained valid after the Revolution. Each rank was denoted by a different combination of epaulette design. Colonels had epaulettes with bullion fringes on both shoulders; majors had epaulettes with bullion fringes but with silver straps; battalion commanders had bullion fringes only on the left epaulette; captains had gold lace fringes only on the left epaulette; adjutants had gold lace fringes only on the right epaulette. Like captains, lieutenants had gold lace fringes only on the left epaulette but with one red stripe on the straps; sub-lieutenants then had two red stripes on the straps; adjutant-NCOs had red straps with two golden stripes and mixed red and gold fringes only on the left epaulette.

While on active service, the officers frequently replaced their coat with a single-breasted tunic without lapels. Known as the surtout or overall, it was entirely dark blue, with red piping on the collar, front and round cuffs. Like the coat, however, it had the epaulettes showing rank on the shoulders.

NCO ranks were shown by diagonal bars of lace applied on the lower sleeves: two orange-yellow bars for corporals, one golden bar piped in red for sergeants, two golden bars piped in red for sergeant-majors. Both NCOs and other ranks had lace service chevrons on the upper sleeves of their coats. These were worn point uppermost and were golden for senior NCOs or red for junior NCOs or rankers. The number of chevrons corresponded to the years of service: one for ten years of service, two for 15 years of service and three for 20 years of service.

Voltigeurs

When the voltigeurs were introduced in 1804, they received a specific uniform that included yellow collar and green epaulettes. Their black bicorn with national cockade had an orange-yellow lace holder and green pompom surmounted by a yellow brush. Their dark blue long-tailed coat with brass buttons had white frontal lapels piped in red, green epaulettes with yellow crescent, yellow collar piped in red, red round cuffs piped in white, white cuff flaps piped in red, white turn-backs piped in red with yellow hunting horns embroidered on the back, horizontal pocket flaps on the back of the coat piped in red and with three buttons. Their outfits were complete with white waistcoat, white trousers, black gaiters during cold months or white gaiters

Above left: **Grenadier of the line infantry in 1805.**

Above right: **Grenadier of the line infantry wearing a bearskin. (Photo: Le Livre, l'Histoire et l'Obusier, © Rose-Hélène Ledanseur)**

during hot months, and black shoes. Yellow became the distinctive colour of the voltigeurs in the same way that red was for the grenadiers.

All the line infantrymen wore loose trousers during regular days and breeches on campaign or on parade. While in their barracks, the NCOs and rankers usually wore only their white waistcoats, which were long-sleeved and single-breasted. These could sometimes have red collar and round cuffs, something that was not prescribed in official regulations. Later, waistcoats started to be worn as campaign dress, especially during hot months in the Mediterranean regions. The waistcoat had two horizontal pocket flaps on the front and two brass buttons on each cuff. When wearing it on campaign, grenadiers and voltigeurs added their distinctive epaulettes to the waistcoat.

Uniforms of the fusiliers; from left to right: fusilier in 1805, fusilier with great coat in 1805, fusilier with 1806 shako, fusilier with great coat and 1810 shako, and fusilier with 1812 dress.

Until 1805, line infantrymen did not receive army regulation great coats and had to wear their own. This changed during 1805–06 when army greatcoats were issued to most regiments for the first time. These were usually single-breasted but could be double-breasted. Their colour was not standardised, since it ranged from beige to brown; grey examples were quite common too. The great coats of officers were usually dark blue. The same epaulettes, rank bars and service chevrons worn on the coat were applied to the greatcoat.

The Shako

In February 1806, there was an important modification to the French line infantry uniforms, when the fusiliers and the voltigeurs replaced their bicorn with a shako. This headgear was distributed to the whole line infantry during 1806–07 and became popular. It had a body made of black felt or board, which widened slightly towards the top, and a waterproofed crown. Around the top and base of the shako there were leather bands that reinforced it; on the front there was a leather peak. A leather chevron was usually applied as strengthening on each side of the headgear. On the front of the top band was a tricolour cockade placed above a lozenge-shaped brass plate that bore an embossed Imperial Eagle and the number of the regiment. The shako was kept in position by brass chinscales that consisted of circular bosses. The first boss on each side, applied on the bottom band of the headgear, was larger than the others and bore a decorative badge (a five-pointed star for fusiliers, a flaming grenade for grenadiers and a hunting horn for voltigeurs). Above the cockade, there was a woollen pompom for fusiliers and a plume for grenadiers and voltigeurs: the pompom was in company colour, the plume of grenadiers was red and the plume of voltigeurs was yellow with a green tip. Wrapped around the shako there were decorative cords and flounders, which were usually removed while on campaign; these were white for fusiliers, red for grenadiers and green for voltigeurs. The shakos of the officers had gold lace on the top band, golden cords/flounders, a golden lace holder for the cockade and gilded fittings.

Sappers

Sapeurs or sappers were dressed like grenadiers, but with a few distinctions: they had a distinctive badge, consisting of two crossed axes, embroidered in red or in white on the sleeves. In addition, the frontal plate of their bearskin did not have the flaming grenade of grenadiers. The sappers carried several exclusive items: white leather gauntlets, white leather apron and white leather axe-case. Beards were mandatory for sappers and were extremely popular among grenadiers.

Line infantry officer with winter great coat and *surtout* tunic.

New Uniforms, 1806

On 25 April 1806, Napoleon decided to change the basic colour of the line infantry uniforms from dark blue to white, thus reverting to the traditional dress of the pre-revolutionary French foot troops. This decision was mostly taken due to economic reasons. As a result of Great Britain's naval blockade of continental Europe, France was cut off from all the major sources of supply of indigo, a key ingredient of dyes used to produce the dark blue cloth of the line infantry uniforms. Initially, the French Ministry of War tried to find domestic substitutes for indigo, but these proved to be inefficient and very expensive. As a result, the Emperor started considering changing the basic colour of the uniforms. After extensive research, white was chosen as the cheapest alternative to dark blue.

On 13 February 1805, Napoleon authorised the trial use of new white uniforms in the third battalions of two infantry regiments: the 18th Line Regiment and the 4th Light Regiment. The Emperor was satisfied with the results of the trial and on 25 April the following year, he decreed the adoption of the new white coats for his entire line infantry, beginning with the following regiments: 3rd, 4th, 8th, 12th, 14th, 15th, 16th, 17th, 18th, 19th, 21st, 22nd, 24th, 25th, 27th, 28th, 32nd, 33rd, 34th and 36th. According to Napoleon's plans, the process of providing new uniforms to the line infantry would be complete by 1809.

The new dress regulations of 1806 introduced an elaborate system for identifying each regiment by using a unique pattern of coloured facings and piping. For this purpose, the line infantry regiments were divided into 14 groups of eight units each; each group was assigned a distinctive facing colour (from the first to the last, in progressive order): dark green, black, scarlet, dark brown, violet, sky blue, pink, light orange, dark blue, yellow, grass green, madder red, crimson and iron grey. Within each of the 14 groups, the first four regiments had yellow metal buttons and horizontal pockets on the back of their coats, while the second four regiments had white metal buttons and vertical pockets on the back of their coats. The units within each of these series of four were differentiated according to the following system: the first wore the distinctive colour on lapels, collar and cuffs; the second wore it on lapels and cuffs; the third wore it on lapels and collar; the fourth wore it on collar and cuffs. Any facing left white was trimmed in the distinctive colour and all the facings being in the distinctive colour were piped in white. The complex system of specifications described above was followed quite closely in the actual manufacturing of the new uniforms. The uniforms retained the same basic cut as the dark blue ones, as well as the distinctive elements prescribed for grenadiers and voltigeurs. The shako was not modified.

Ultimately, only 12 of the 20 regiments that had been selected to receive the new dress replaced their dark blue uniforms with white ones. The opposition of the officers and soldiers to the new dress was strong, since the French line infantrymen had always been proud of their national uniforms. White was the colour of the old – and hated – royal army. It was also the colour worn by Austrian infantrymen, who had been enemies of France for decades.

The critical test of the new white uniform came soon after its adoption by the first 12 regiments and was a failure. During the Prussian campaign of 1806 and the Polish campaign of 1807, the white coats proved to be impossible to keep clean. Blood showed up vividly on them, affecting the morale of their wearers. On the march, the white coats were soon covered with dust and mud. These new uniforms became soiled so easily that they were uneconomical; the dark blue coats had been more expensive to produce than the white ones, but were more durable. As a result, on 23 May 1806, Napoleon halted the distribution of the new dress and in October, he ordered production of dark blue coats to begin again. The regiments that had received the new white uniforms were to continue using them until they wore out; as a result, the French line infantry continued to include some regiments dressed in the white until 1809.

Uniforms of the line infantry grenadiers; from left to right: grenadier with bearskin, grenadier with 1810 shako, and grenadier with 1812 dress.

1810 Shako

The dark blue uniforms of the French line infantry remained unchanged until 9 November 1810, when a new model of shako was introduced. It was slightly taller and more robust than the previous one; it did not have chevrons on the sides and did not have cords/flounders. The original shako, however, continued to be worn by most of the regiments. The new shako was to have a pompom instead of the plume for grenadiers and for voltigeurs, but this feature was never adopted. The grenadiers simply added a red pompom to the base of their red plumes and the voltigeurs added a yellow pompom to the base of their yellow-tipped green plumes. The frontal plate of the new shako was lozenge-shaped and bore the distinctive number of each regiment; several units, however, used a different kind of brass plate that was crescent-shaped and bore an Imperial Eagle. This alternative design, which was not prescribed by official regulations, became so popular that it was officially adopted with the new dress regulations of 1812.

In February 1811, the system of pompoms and plumes of the headgear was regularised as follows: colonels had to wear an entirely white plume, majors had to wear a white-over-red plume, battalion commanders had to wear an entirely red plume, and all other officers and the NCOs of the regimental staff were to have white pompoms. Grenadiers had a red pompom, voltigeurs a yellow one. Each of the four fusilier companies that comprised a line infantry battalion wore pompoms in a different colour: dark green for the 1st Company, sky blue for 2nd, orange for 3rd and violet for 4th. Sometimes the pompom could bear the battalion number in white and could be surmounted by a tuft in its same colour; these variations, however, were not permitted according to official dress regulations. On the new shako, introduced during 1810, the golden top band worn by officers had a different width according to rank.

On campaign, the harsh conditions of life of the common soldiers impacted their clothing. Loose trousers or overalls were extremely common; they could be grey, ochre, brown or dark blue according to the materials available locally. Shako covers were used by most of the soldiers to protect their precious headgear. These were made of black waterproof fabric or of buff cotton. The covers concealed most of the decorations, except for the pompom/plume. Sometimes regimental numbers or regimental badges could be painted on the front of these covers. During long marches, trousers were turned up at the hem, or were tied around the ankle with string; the great coat was frequently worn directly over the waistcoat and the dark blue coat was carried in the knapsack.

Musicians

Until the 1812 dress regulations were adopted, the uniforms of musicians were governed by the personal tastes of the colonels commanding single regiments. The members of the regimental band wore coats in extravagant colours, such as red or yellow. Often these were worn with non-regulation headgear such as bicorns adorned with ostrich feathers or *czapkas* (square-topped cavalry caps typical of the Polish lancers). The uniforms of the regimental bands were a triumph of colours: their facings were all trimmed with multi-colour lace, they had trefoil-shaped epaulettes in the same colour as the trimming and sometimes included decorative shoulder wings that were worn under the epaulettes. Trousers could be decorated on the front with embroidered knots, while the standard leg-wear was usually replaced with black leather half-boots having coloured top edging and front tassel. The plumes, pompoms, cords and flounders of their shakos could be in many different colours (usually matching the coat or its trimming).

Drum-majors had the most ornate uniforms: these usually comprised a black bicorn trimmed with golden lace and featuring massive plumes usually in the three colours of the French flag. They also had leather gauntlets and a laced baldric made of cloth to support their ornamental sabre. Their most important mark of distinction, however, was the corded mace that was used to direct the regimental band. In most cases, the trimming of the drum-majors' uniforms were golden, like the epaulettes worn on their shoulders. As an alternative to the bicorn, these veteran musicians could have a busby made of fur that was very similar to that worn by the contemporary French light cavalry.

Drum-corporals were dressed like drum-majors, but with less decoration. The musicians of the single companies – drummers for fusiliers, fifers for grenadiers and hornists for voltigeurs – were dressed in a much simpler way and looked more like their comrades. They had coloured lacing on the facings, on the pockets and on the turn-backs; in addition, they usually had decorative stripes of coloured lace applied on the sleeves and coloured 'shoulder-wings'. Shako ornaments, company distinctions, badges on the turn-backs and epaulettes matched those worn by regular soldiers.

1812 Bardin Regulations

On 19 January 1812, new dress regulations were introduced and remained in use until the fall of Napoleon in 1815. They were named after Major Bardin, who was responsible for their issue. They retained the general features and colours of the national dress uniform but introduced important modifications. The old coat was replaced with a double-breasted and short-tailed dark blue jacket known as a habit-veste. It had plastron-style lapels on the front and vertical pockets on the back. The white short turn-backs of the new uniform bore a dark blue crowned 'N' for fusiliers, a red flaming grenade for grenadiers, and a yellow hunting horn for voltigeurs.

Fusiliers had dark blue shoulder straps piped in red, while grenadiers had red epaulettes, and voltigeurs had yellow epaulettes with green crescents (this did not change from the previous uniform). Rank distinctions and service chevrons remained unchanged. The white waistcoat, which was no longer visible, now had a lower collar and coloured shoulder straps (dark blue for fusiliers, red for grenadiers and yellow for voltigeurs). The black or white gaiters no longer extended over the knee.

The 1812 dress regulations also introduced a new model of shako, with a new kind of brass frontal plate that bore a crowned Imperial Eagle atop a semi-circular plate into which the regimental number was cut. The new shako had decorative brass finials; these reproduced a lion-head for fusiliers, a flaming grenade for grenadiers and a hunting horn for voltigeurs. The usual tricolour cockade and brass chinscales of the previous model of shako were retained; cords and flounders were officially abolished, but in practice they continued to be worn by most of the regiments. The bearskins of the grenadiers were made obsolete and thus grenadier companies started to wear shakos. Grenadiers' shakos had red top and bottom bands as well as red side-chevrons; voltigeurs' shakos had yellow top and bottom bands as well as yellow side chevrons. The shakos of the fusiliers had tufted pompoms in company colours, while those of the elite companies had a tufted pompom and plume in red for grenadiers or green tufted pompom and green plume tipped in yellow for voltigeurs.

The Bardin Regulations introduced a new model of forage cap that replaced the previous bonnet de police; this was known as a *pokalem* and was a pied-shaped dark blue cap with a folding neckflap that could be fastened under the chin. The pokalem was piped in red and bore the regimental number or the grenadier/voltigeur badge embroidered in red on the front.

As a result of all the changes, the new uniform of a fusilier according to the 1812 dress regulations was: black shako with black top and bottom bands, brass chinscales and frontal plate, national cockade and pompom in company colours; dark blue habit-

Above left: **Grenadier of the line infantry with 1812 dress.**
(Photo: 33ème Regiment d'Infanterie de Ligne, © Katarzyna Pucyło)

Above right: **Grenadier of the line infantry with winter greatcoat.**

Above left: **NCO of the line infantry voltigeurs wearing bicorn. (Photo: Voltigeurs of the 18th Line Regiment, © Jan Štábl)**

Above right: **Privates of the line infantry voltigeurs wearing summer campaign dress. (Photo: Voltigeurs of the 18th Line Regiment, © Jan Štábl)**

veste with red collar and round cuffs piped in white, dark blue shoulder straps piped in red, dark blue cuff flaps piped in red, white frontal plastron piped in red, brass buttons, white short turn-backs piped in red with embroidered company badge, dark blue vertical pocket flaps piped in red on the back of the jacket, white trousers, black or white gaiters.

Grenadiers had plume, pompom, side-chevrons, top and bottom bands of the shako in red; in addition, they wore red fringed epaulettes.

Voltigeurs had side-chevrons, top and bottom bands of the shako in yellow; their pompom was green and their plume was green tipped in yellow. In addition, they wore green epaulettes with yellow crescents and the collar of their jacket was yellow with dark blue piping.

Uniforms of the line infantry voltigeurs; from left to right: voltigeur in 1804, voltigeurs with 1806 shako and voltigeur with 1812 dress.

The Bardin Regulations attempted to regularise the uniforms of the musicians by introducing a standardised imperial livery that had to be worn by all. This consisted of a dark green single-breasted jacket decorated with stripes of lace having alternate yellow and green segments. The yellow segments were decorated with an interwoven dark green crowned 'N', while the dark green segments were decorated with an interwoven yellow Imperial Eagle.

Drum-majors were to have double silver lace on the collar, while general musicians had the same decorative lace that was on the jacket added to the collar and cuffs. Both collar and cuffs were red; cuff flaps and shoulder straps were dark green with red piping. Despite the promulgation of the new dress regulations, however, many bands continued to wear their previous regimental distinctions (such as busby hats or coloured trousers) of which they were particularly fond. During the brief restoration of the Bourbons in 1814, some elements of the line infantry uniforms were modified: the tricolour cockade was replaced by the old white one, a new shako plate bearing the coat of arms of the royal family came into use and the 'N' badges were removed from the turn-backs of the fusiliers' jackets.

EQUIPMENT

The standard equipment of the French line infantrymen was consistent during 1799–1815. It included the following basic elements: a knapsack with a closing flap made of calfskin, to be carried on the back using buff leather shoulder straps, secured with metal buckles. A black leather cartridge box was constructed to receive cartridges. It had an external flap with a brass badge applied to its exterior identifying the regimental number for fusiliers, flaming grenade for grenadiers and hunting horn for voltigeurs. Included in the inventory was one whitened buff leather crossbelt to which the cartridge box was suspended and one whitened buff leather crossbelt to which the bayonet scabbard was suspended. The cartridge box sat on the right hip, the bayonet scabbard on the left. The great coat was transported on top of the knapsack and was kept in position with three white leather straps closed with metal buckles. The fatigue cap was attached to the bottom part of the cartridge box. The bayonet scabbard was made of black leather and had brass fittings.

Grenadiers and voltigeurs also carried a short sword, which was fastened together with the bayonet scabbard; the scabbard

NCO of the line infantry voltigeurs wearing shako with protective oilskin cover. (Photo: Voltigeurs of the 18th Line Regiment, © Jan Štábl)

was made of black leather with brass fittings. In addition, non-regulation pieces of equipment were carried. These included canteens and canvas satchels of various dimensions. Canteens could be wooden barrels, bottles with wicker-work cases, or metal flasks suspended on a coloured cord. On campaign, especially in the Iberian Peninsula, dried pumpkins were often transformed into rudimental canteens.

The standard weapon of the French line infantry was the M1777 Charleville musket, a smoothbore flintlock of 17.5mm calibre with iron fittings. It was 151.5cm long and weighed 4.375kg. Voltigeurs sometimes carried a shortened version of this weapon that was produced specifically for the cavalry dragoons. The bayonet of the Charleville musket was 45.6cm long and triangular in section. Grenadiers and voltigeurs were also armed with an infantry sabre-briquet or short sword, which had a cast-brass hilt and a curved guard ending in a pyramidal or rounded quillon. The blade of this weapon was curved like that of a cavalry sabre. The sword knot of the sabre-briquet was white for fusiliers, red for grenadiers, and green with a yellow tassel for voltigeurs. Officers carried a straight-bladed sword with single-bar guard and helmet-shaped pommel, which was suspended on a shoulder belt or a waistbelt passing beneath the front flap of the breeches. The scabbard of this elegant weapon was made of black leather and had gilded metal fittings. The sword knots of officers were golden.

Chapter 2

Light Infantry

HISTORY AND ORGANISATION

During the Napoleonic period, the line and light regiments of the French infantry performed similar tactical duties on the battlefield; only the voltigeur companies were true light infantrymen. The regiments of light infantry were more intensively trained in marksmanship than line infantry and were able to execute standard infantry manoeuvres with higher speed. During large pitched battles, they were mostly employed in lines, or in columns, in the same manner as the regiments of fusiliers. The chasseurs of the light regiments formed advance guards or scouting parties in front of the line units during marches. This task was performed by soldiers who were able to judge the tactical situation independently from the orders received. In most cases, the light infantry regiments had a superior military reputation to the line infantry ones.

According to contemporary observers, no light infantry corps in Europe was able to fight more effectively than the French one in open order. More agile and with better marksmen than the fusiliers, the chasseurs proved to be effective when fighting over densely wooded areas, or in urban centres, where the line infantry usually experienced more difficulties in being deployed. Physical fitness and boldness were key factors behind the success of the French light infantrymen, together with the flexibility of their units.

Each company of chasseurs could be divided into three small sections when skirmishing. The left and right sections were tasked with firing upon the enemies from covert positions and had the bayonets removed from their muskets in order to be more agile. The centre section was deployed in line, with bayonets fixed, and was to act as a 'screen' behind which the other two sections could fall for protection in case of need.

When skirmishing with the enemy, the French chasseurs had officers and artillerymen as their primary targets: the former gave orders to the rank and file and thus played a critical role on the battlefield; the latter were specialised soldiers and could not be easily replaced with standard infantrymen in their functions.

In the Allied armies that fought against France, officers were more important than their French equivalents, since the Allied soldiers were not able to act independently without orders from their officers, unlike the French ones. As a result, killing the officers of an enemy unit meant paralysing the unit on the battlefield.

Firing at enemy artillerymen also had a great tactical advantage, since killing gunners was much easier than capturing or destroying enemy guns. An attack could be made from a distance and without losing soldiers, whereas capturing or destroying artillery pieces could only be achieved by launching frontal charges. It should be remembered, however, that the French chasseurs were all armed with the standard muskets of the line infantry. These were heavy smoothbores with poor rates of accuracy from a distance. As a result, the performance of Napoleon's light infantrymen was due to their great determination and training rather than the quality of their personal equipment.

In several Allied armies, the light infantry was equipped with rifled carbines, which gave them a significant technological advantage over the French light regiments. However, no other military power in Europe had as many light infantry units as France.

Above left: Sergeant major of the line infantry voltigeurs wearing 1812 dress in Spain. The brown loose trousers were typical of campaign uniforms.

Above right: Voltigeurs of the line infantry wearing winter great coat. (Photo by Le Livre, l'Histoire et l'Obusier, © Rose-Hélène Ledanseur)

As in the pre-1789 years, French chasseurs continued to be mostly recruited from mountainous regions. The communities living in the French mountains produced a high percentage of hunters trained in their childhoods and who were used to moving very rapidly on broken terrain. As a result, volunteers and recruits coming from the Alps and Pyrenees were usually assigned to the light infantry regiments.

Napoleon always paid great attention to the training of his light infantry corps, but on several occasions he was obliged to employ them as standard line infantry. When deployed in line or in column, the French light infantrymen exhibited all their valour and courage.

In 1799, the French infantry comprised a total of 30 light demi-brigades numbered from 1 to 30. Each consisted of three battalions, which by now had an homogenous quality in terms of training and experience.

- A single battalion consisted of one carabinier company and nine chasseur companies.
- Chasseurs of the light units corresponded to fusiliers of the line units and the carabiniers of the light units corresponded to grenadiers of the line units.
- A single company consisted of the following elements: one captain, one lieutenant, one sub-lieutenant, one sergeant-major, five sergeants, one corporal-fourrier, eight corporals, two hornists and 104 privates.
- The elite carabinier companies had a similar structure, but with four sergeants and 64 privates.
- The regimental staff of each half-brigade comprised one colonel, three battalion commanders, one adjutant, one paymaster, one drum-major, three standard-bearers, one surgeon, four assistant-surgeons, one shoemaker, one gaiter-maker, one gunsmith, one tailor and eight musicians.

In 1803, Napoleon was obliged to reconsider the general structure of his light infantry since several regiments had to be disbanded following the French defeat in Haiti. As a result of that debacle, Napoleon disbanded four light infantry regiments, the 11th, 19th, 20th and 30th, with their designations remaining vacant after that time. Due to this action, the French light infantry comprised 26 regiments in December 1803. During 1804, however, a new 31st Light Regiment was created from the remnants of the four units that had been disbanded during the previous year.

In 1804, Napoleon introduced voltigeurs to his light infantry battalions, so as to have specialised skirmishers in the chasseur regiments. Instead of adding more soldiers to each battalion, and in order to retain the standard number of ten companies for each unit, Napoleon ordered that the second company of chasseurs in each light infantry battalion re-train its members to become a voltigeur company. These were an elite sub-unit, like the carabinier company, that was already included in each battalion. From 1804, each light infantry battalion started to include two elite companies and eight chasseur companies. Over time, the voltigeur companies found themselves detached – quite frequently – from the parent battalions to form temporary ad hoc battalions of elite skirmishers. These were employed to conduct special operations, such as storming enemy positions or conducting long-range scouting missions.

When a light infantry battalion was deployed in line on the battlefield, the carabinier company was placed on the right and the voltigeur company was placed on the left of its formation; as a result, the two elite companies were also known as 'flank companies' to differentiate them from the central chasseurs. Generally, the carabiniers were chosen from the tallest and strongest recruits assigned to each battalion while the voltigeurs were chosen from the smallest men since they had to move very rapidly. In addition, both carabiniers and voltigeurs usually had some combat experience, since they were chosen from veterans who had already served for a few years.

After 1804, the general structure of the French light infantry saw no significant changes until 1808: these were the years of Napoleon's greatest victories and of the proclamation of the Empire. The French light infantrymen showed their valour in a series of memorable pitched battles: Ulm, Austerlitz, Jena, Auerstadt, Eylau and Friedland. The French chasseurs were well disciplined and could adapt to any tactical situation. They had no fear of launching frontal bayonet assaults and also knew how to skirmish on any kind of terrain.

On 18 February 1808, Napoleon partly modified the organisation of his light infantry, by enlarging it but without creating new regiments. In his reforms, each light infantry regiment was to consist of four active battalions – known as bataillons de guerre – plus one smaller depot battalion, which would consist of just four chasseur companies.

- A single bataillon de guerre was to comprise one company of carabiniers, one company of voltigeurs and four companies of chasseurs.
- A light infantry regiment was to have four companies of carabiniers, four companies of voltigeurs, 16 companies of chasseurs and four depot companies. The depot was tasked with providing new recruits to the bataillons de guerre as replacements.
- The regimental staff of each regiment was to consist of one colonel, one major, four battalion commanders, five adjutants, five assistants, ten sergeant-majors, one drum-major, one drum-corporal, one band-master, seven musicians, four craftsmen, one quartermaster, one paymaster, one surgeon-major and four assistant-surgeons.

Unlike the line regiments, the light regiments did not have regimental standard-bearers. Instead, one battalion standard was awarded to each of the four active battalions that made up a chasseur regiment. The battalions of the light regiments had to serve as detached and independent units on most occasions and so there was no need to assign a single Imperial Eagle to the whole regiment. The commander of each light battalion was to choose one veteran NCO from the companies under his command to carry the battalion standard.

- A single light infantry company comprised one captain, one lieutenant, one sub-lieutenant, one sergeant-major, four sergeants, one corporal-quartermaster, eight corporals, two hornists and 121 privates.

The carabinier companies and the voltigeur companies had this standard formation. Carabiniers had to be chosen from the soldiers who already had four years of service and who had participated to at least two of the following battles: Ulm, Austerlitz, Jena and Friedland. A carabinier had to be at least 173.5cm tall. Voltigeurs had to be chosen from the soldiers who already had two years of service; they could not be taller than 150cm. Both the carabiniers and the voltigeurs received higher pay than the chasseurs, due to their elite status.

The depot battalion was commanded by a major and was not sent to the front in case of war. Each of its four companies had a different function: the 4th Company never left the depot and was mostly tasked with outfitting and training the new recruits. Attached to the 4th Company there were the so-called 'enfants de troupe' – sons or orphans of soldiers who were on the battalion's payroll – and the veteran soldiers who were awaiting retirement or pensioning. It was assisted by a dressing captain and by a quartermaster-treasurer. The 1st and 3rd Company were responsible

Above left: **Officer of the line infantry wearing 1806 'experimental' white uniform.**

Above right: **Fusilier of the line infantry wearing 1806 'experimental' white uniform.**

for transferring the newly trained recruits to the active battalions; the 2nd Company was generally employed to perform garrison duties in the various military facilities.

The four *bataillons de guerre* of each regiment included four sappers each, who were attached to the carabinier company and who were under command of the pioneer corporal (there was one such NCO for each regiment). The sappers were to act as combat engineers: their main task was to build field fortifications as well as to remove obstacles that could be encountered by the battalion during the march. Sappers had the same status and privileges as the carabiniers.

The internal organisation of the French light infantry units introduced in 1808 remained practically unchanged until the end of the Napoleonic Period in 1815.

Raising New Regiments

During the years 1805–15, the general establishment of the French light infantry troops was increased through the formation of new units. The first to be created was the 32nd Light Regiment, which came into existence during 1805. It was formed by assembling the two infantry battalions of the army of the Ligurian Republic. This region was a French puppet state from 1797, then annexed to the Empire in 1805 when its small military forces were absorbed into the French Army. The two Ligurian battalions, despite being line units, already had a distinct light infantry character.

In 1810, the Kingdom of Holland, which was ruled by Napoleon's brother, Louis Bonaparte, as a puppet state of France from 1806, was annexed to the Empire and, from that point, its armed forces were absorbed into the French Army. With this additional resource, the French light infantry could raise the new 33rd Light Regiment. A unit bearing this denomination had already existed during 1808–09, but it had been a temporary corps created for service in the Iberian Peninsula and was soon disbanded. In 1809, Napoleon formed seven temporary auxiliary battalions by assembling different detachments of line infantry regiments that were already serving in the Iberian Peninsula. Then, in 1811, these battalions were formed two new regular regiments (one of line infantry and one of light infantry). The 1st, 3rd and 6th Auxiliary Battalions became the 130th Line Regiment; the 2nd, 4th, 5th and 7th Auxiliary Battalions became the 34th Light Regiment.

In 1811, Napoleon raised again the 11th Light Regiment, previously disbanded in 1803, y assembling four special/foreign battalions): the Tirailleurs Corses (from Corsica), the Tirailleurs du Po (from the former Duchy of Parma), the Tirailleurs de la Légion du Midi (from Piedmont), and the Valaisan Battalion (from Switzerland). Despite its composite nature, the new 11th Light Regiment proved to be an effective unit.

On 8 June 1808, following the annexation of Tuscany to the Empire, Napoleon ordered the organisation of a new regiment to be made up of conscripts from the new Italian departments that had resisted conscription. This semi-penal unit had a light infantry character from its foundation and became a regiment in 1810 (with five battalions). Its official denomination was 1st Mediterranean Regiment. In March 1811, a 2nd Mediterranean Regiment of the same kind was organised, but this was soon absorbed into the French line infantry as the 133rd Regiment. In 1812, the 1st Mediterranean Regiment was absorbed into the French infantry as the 35th Light Regiment.

By 1812, a new 36th Light Regiment was added to the general structure of the chasseur units. Following Britain's blockade of continental Europe's coasts, Napoleon organised local infantry battalions to protect his Empire's most exposed tracts of coastline. In particular, he was keen to protect small islands of the French territory that could be attacked and seized by the Royal Navy. As a result, in 1810, three battalions were formed on three small islands: the Battalion of Belle Ile, the Batallion of Ile de Ré, and the Battalion of Walcheren.

Belle Ile is located along the southern coast of Brittany; Ile de Ré is located in front of La Rochelle in Aquitaine, and Walcheren is located on the coast of Zealand (in the Netherlands, which had been annexed by France). All the three islands were extremely important from a naval point of view and their capture by the British was to be avoided at all costs. In 1809, a British expeditionary corps had occupied Walcheren for several weeks and Napoleon had learned from that experience. In 1811, the Battalion of Belle Ile was transformed into a regiment by absorbing Italian conscripts who had initially been assigned to the 2nd Mediterranean Regiment and thus could be enlarged to an establishment of five battalions. In 1812, due to its good conduct, the Regiment of Belle Ile was absorbed into the French infantry as the 36th Light Regiment.

On 7 February 1812, some weeks before the beginning of the Russian campaign, a 37th Light Regiment was created by assembling several detachments from garrison battalions of existing chasseur regiments. In December 1813, Napoleon raised a new 19th Light Regiment, previously disbanded in 1803. The revived unit was formed by assembling remnants of several battalions that had returned from the disastrous Russian campaign, including the 4th Battalion of the 1st Light Regiment, the 3rd Battalion of the 3rd Light Regiment, the 1st Battalion of the 22nd Light Regiment, the 2nd Battalion of the 22nd Light Regiment and the 1st Battalion of the 35th Light Regiment.

Following the first abdication of Napoleon on 12 May 1814, the restored monarchy reduced the number of light infantry regiments. The chasseur units were reduced to 15 (numbered from 1 to 15, without vacancies). When Napoleon returned from exile in 1815, the new structure remained, though he restored the old numbering system retaining vacant numbers. Generally, the reduction ordered by the restored monarchy in 1814 was positive, since by dissolving the most inexperienced regiments, the remaining 15 could fill their ranks with the best elements of the disbanded units.

Colonel of the line infantry wearing 1812 uniform.

UNIFORMS

In 1799, the French light infantry was dressed in the national uniform introduced in 1793. It was similar to that worn by the line infantry but was medium blue instead of dark blue, with some decorative elements in medium blue (such as the frontal lapels of the coat and on the waistcoat and trousers).

The standard uniform of a chasseur in 1799 was: black bicorn with tricolour national cockade and half-green and half-red woollen tuft. Men wore a medium blue short-tailed coat with red collar and round cuffs piped in white. The medium blue lapels, shoulder straps, turn-backs, and vertical pocket flaps on the back of the coat, as well as the red cuff flaps were all piped white. Three buttons on the back pocket flaps and brass buttons on the front completed the coat. In addition, each soldier had a medium blue waistcoat, medium blue trousers, black half-boots with white piping at the top and a white tassel on the front.

Carabiniers wore the same dress but incorporated distinctive elements used by the line infantry's grenadiers. These included red-fringed epaulettes in place of the standard shoulder straps and a black bearskin cap as headgear. The latter had a tricolour cockade, red cords and flounders, red plume and red crown with a white cross. To distinguish them from the grenadiers, the bearskins of the carabiniers did not have the brass frontal plate. The cuffs of the coat could be pointed in some cases and the cuff-flaps worn by officers/NCOs could sometimes have a different shape; these were the most common non-regulation features that could be found on light infantry uniforms. These variations derived from the fact that uniforms were produced locally. Over time, non-regulation details became much rarer as Napoleon sought to dress his soldiers in a consistent style.

Other non-regulation modifications included the lack of white piping on the frontal lapels, and the use of horizontal pocket flaps on the back of the coat (instead of the vertical ones prescribed by regulations). The turn-backs could feature embroidered company badges such as white hunting horns for chasseurs and red flaming grenades for carabiniers. Over time, most of the regiments started to substitute their original brass buttons for white metal examples, which bore a hunting horn and the regimental number. The waistcoat had to be single-breasted according to official regulations, but it was not uncommon to find double-breasted versions; it had to be medium blue, but red and white ones were also quite popular. From 1800, the standard shoulder straps of the chasseurs were sometimes replaced with non-regulation green epaulettes with or without red crescents. The piping and tassel on the half-boots was specified as white for chasseurs and red for carabiniers, but it was not uncommon for them to be green.

A few features of the uniform were slightly modified at a later date. The coat tails were shortened in order to be more practical, and the frontal lapels started to have an accentuated curve. According to official regulations, the trousers of the light infantry had to be medium blue, but white trousers were quite popular during hot months. On 26 October 1801, the black bicorn was replaced – for the light infantry regiments – with the shako. Some chasseur units had already been wearing non-regulation shakos well before 1801. These were of the so-called 'mirliton' type, which imitated contemporary light cavalry fashions and consisted of a cloth 'wing' that was wrapped around the body of a tall peak-less cap. The tall cap was black and the cloth wing was usually green or yellow. Positioned on the left side of the cap would be a half-yellow and half-green plume in addition to the national cockade, and the wing could have a green or yellow tassel at its end.

The shako introduced by the 1801 dress regulations was the direct heir of this non-regulation mirliton headgear, but it did not feature the cloth wing. In shape, it was quite squat but widened slightly towards the top; on the front, it had a detachable peak that was set a short way up the body of the cap. The peak was fastened by hooks and eyes. Sometimes the plume and cockade of the shako could be fixed on the front of it and not on the left side, since the peak of the headgear could be detached. The shako was constructed of black felt and featured black leather top and bottom bands. A brass badge shaped like a hunting horn was placed on the front. On the left side, the national cockade was secured by an orange-yellow lace holder. Wrapped around the headgear were green decorative cords and flounders; on the left side of the shako was a drooping plume in green for chasseurs and in red for carabiniers. The top and bottom bands of the carabiniers' shakos were red with red cords and flounders and the brass badge on the front depicted a flaming grenade. Following the introduction of the shako, bearskins of the carabiniers were worn only for parade or combat, thus becoming much rarer to see.

Line infantry conscripts during the French campaign of 1814; they are all wearing the new pokalem fatigue cap.

Voltigeurs

When the voltigeurs were introduced in 1804, they received a specific uniform. Their black shako had a brass frontal plate, yellow cords and flounders, black top and bottom bands, black peak, national cockade, and a half-yellow and half-green plume. They wore a medium blue short-tailed coat with yellow collar piped with white. Its medium blue round cuffs and frontal lapels were piped with white. It had green epaulettes decorated with a red crescent. On the back of the coat, the medium blue vertical pocket flaps were piped with white and featuring three white metal buttons. The medium blue turn-backs on the tails were piped with white and featured yellow hunting horn badges. The outfit was complete with medium blue waistcoat, medium blue trousers, black half-boots with yellow piping on the top and yellow tassel on the front.

Some non-regulation variations of this dress did exist: the yellow collar could be piped with red, the cuff flaps could be yellow instead of red, and the cuffs could be pointed instead of rounded. The piping

Grenadier (left) and officer (right) of the line infantry with the provisional uniform worn during the restoration of 1814. Note the use of white cockades instead of the tricolour ones.

Chasseurs of the light infantry in 1804; they are all wearing 1801 shako.

and tassel on the half-boots and the cords and flounders of the shako could be white or green. During 1804–06, several companies of voltigeurs replaced their shakos with non-regulation busby hats made of brown or black fur, copying those worn by the light cavalry. These had yellow 'bags' of cloth on the back and a half-yellow and half-green plume; sometimes they were worn by the carabinier companies, with red 'bags' of cloth on the back and a red plume.

All the light infantrymen wore loose trousers daily and breeches on campaign or on parade. While in their barracks, the NCOs and rankers usually wore only medium blue waistcoats, which were long-sleeved and single-breasted. These could sometimes have red collar and round cuffs. The waistcoat had two horizontal pocket flaps on the front and two white metal buttons on each cuff; when these were worn on campaign, grenadiers and voltigeurs added their distinctive epaulettes to the waistcoat.

Until 1805, in winter, neither the line nor the light infantry received great coats and wore their own civilian overcoats or cloaks. During 1805–06, army great coats were issued to most regiments. These were usually single-breasted but could be double-breasted. Their colour was not standardised, since it ranged from beige to brown; grey examples were quite common. The great coats of officers were usually dark blue. The light infantrymen used the bonnet de police as an undress cap: this was medium blue with white piping and had a tasselled stocking end folded up and tucked behind the right-hand side of a stiffened headband. The tassel was white, and on the front of the cap there was a red flaming grenade for carabinier companies.

According to the egalitarian principles of the Revolution, officers were dressed exactly like their men, but their uniforms were of finer material. When compared with those of NCOs and rankers, they had longer tails to their waistcoats. The officers' shakos had silver frontal plates and silver cords/flounders; their top band was decorated in the form of silver laurel leaves or of silver interlocking rings embroidered on a black velvet backing. Officers wore a gilt *gorget* under their neck, which was mostly used on parade and incorporated decorative silver devices that usually included unit number and – after 1804 – an Imperial Eagle.

Officers displayed their rank with silver lace epaulettes that were worn on the shoulders. Each rank was decorated with a different combination on the epaulettes. Colonels had epaulettes with bullion fringes on both shoulders; majors had epaulettes with bullion fringes but with silver straps; battalion commanders had bullion fringes only on the left epaulette; captains had gold lace fringes only on the left epaulette; adjutants had gold lace fringes only on the right epaulette; lieutenants had the same as captains but with one red stripe on the straps; likewise sub-lieutenants had two red stripes on the straps; adjutant-NCOs had red straps with two golden stripes and mixed red-and-gold fringes only on the left epaulette.

While on active service, the officers frequently replaced their coat with a single-breasted tunic without lapels known as a surtout or overall. This was entirely medium blue, with white piping on the collar, front and round cuffs. Like the coat, however, it had the epaulettes showing rank on the shoulders. NCO ranks were shown by diagonal bars of lace that applied on the lower sleeves: two white bars for corporals, one silver bar piped in red for sergeants, two silver bars piped in red for sergeant-majors. Both NCOs and rankers had lace service chevrons on the upper sleeves of their coats; these were worn point uppermost and were silver for senior NCOs or red for junior NCOs and rankers. The number of chevrons corresponded to the years of service: one for ten years of service, two for 15 years and three for 20 years of service. The same epaulettes, rank bars and service chevrons worn on the coat were applied to the great coat.

In February 1806, there was an important modification to the uniforms of the French infantry,

Officer of the light infantry with 1806 shako.

when a new model of shako was introduced for line and light regiments. The new headgear had a body made of black felt or board, which widened slightly towards its top, and a waterproof crown. Around the top and the bottom of the shako there were leather bands for reinforcement, and on the front there was a leather peak. A leather chevron was usually applied as strengthening on each side of the headgear. On the front of the top band there was a tricolour cockade placed above a lozenge-shaped brass plate that bore an embossed Imperial Eagle and the number of the regiment. The shako was kept in position by brass chinscales that consisted of circular bosses; the first boss on each side, applied on the bottom band of the headgear, was larger than the others and bore a decorative badge (a hunting horn for chasseurs and voltigeurs, or a flaming grenade for carabiniers). Above the cockade there was a woollen pompom for chasseurs and a plume for carabiniers and voltigeurs: the pompom was in company colour, the plume of carabiniers was red and the plume of voltigeurs was yellow with a green tip. Wrapped around the shako there were decorative cords and flounders, which were usually removed while on campaign; these were white for chasseurs, red for carabiniers and green for voltigeurs. The shakos of the officers had silver lace on the top band, silver cords/flounders, a silver lace holder for the cockade and gilded fittings. With the introduction of the new shako in 1806, the bearskin of the carabiniers was discontinued, but was retained by some companies during the following years.

Sappers

Sapeurs, or sappers, continued to be dressed in the same way as the carabiniers for the whole period taken into account, but with a few distinctions: they had a distinctive badge, consisting of two crossed axes embroidered in red or in white on the sleeves. The sappers retained their bearskin after 1806, which could be replaced by a smaller busby. They carried several specific pieces of equipment: white leather gauntlets, white leather apron and white leather axe-case. Beards were mandatory for sappers and were also extremely popular among carabiniers. Other than the 4th Light Regiment, the light infantry units were not affected by the introduction of the 1806 white experimental dress.

The medium blue uniforms of the French light infantry remained unchanged until 9 November 1810, when a new model of shako was introduced. This was slightly taller and more robust than the previous one; it did not have chevrons on the sides and did not have cords/flounders, although these continued to be worn by most of the regiments. The new shako was to have a pompom for carabiniers and for voltigeurs instead of the plume, but this feature was never adopted: the carabiniers simply added a red pompom to the base of their red plumes and the voltigeurs added a yellow pompom to the base of their yellow plumes tipped in green. The frontal plate of the new shako was a lozenge and bore the distinctive number of each regiment inside a hunting horn for chasseurs/voltigeurs and inside a flaming grenade for carabiniers. Several units, however, used a different kind of brass plate that was crescent-shaped and bore an Imperial Eagle. This design was prescribed by official regulations but became so popular that it was officially adopted with the new dress regulations of 1812.

In February 1811, the system of pompoms and plumes of the headgear was regularised. Colonels had to wear an entirely white plume, majors had to wear a white-over-red plume and battalion commanders had to wear an entirely red plume; all other officers and the NCOs of the regimental staff were to have white pompoms. Carabiniers had a red pompom, voltigeurs a yellow one. Each of the four chasseur companies that comprised a light infantry battalion wore pompoms in a different colour, which varied for each regiment. Sometimes the pompom could bear the battalion number in white and could be surmounted by a tuft in its same colour; these variations, however, were not permitted according to official dress regulations.

On the new shako, introduced during 1810, the silver top band worn by officers was of a different width according to rank. Shako covers were used by most of the soldiers, in order to protect their precious headgear; these were made of black waterproof fabric or of buff cotton. The covers concealed most of the shako's decorations, except for the pompom/plume. Sometimes, regimental numbers or regimental badges could be painted on the front of these covers.

On campaign, loose trousers or overalls were extremely common. They could be grey, ochre, brown or medium blue according to the clothing materials available locally. During long marches, the trousers were turned up at the bottom or were tied around the ankle with string; the great coat was frequently worn directly over the waistcoat and the medium blue coat was carried in the knapsack.

Light Infantry Musicians

Until the 1812 dress regulations were enforced, the uniforms of the light infantry musicians were governed by the personal tastes of the colonels commanding the single regiments. The members of the regimental band wore coats in extravagant colours, such as yellow or green. Frequently they were worn with non-regulation headgear such as bicorns adorned with ostrich feathers, or with *czapkas* (square-topped cavalry caps typical of the Polish lancers). The uniforms of the regimental bandsmen were a triumph of colours: their facings were trimmed with multi-colour lace. They had trefoil-shaped epaulettes in the same colour as the trimming and sometimes incorporated decorative shoulder wings worn under the epaulettes. Trousers could be decorated on the front with embroidered knots, while the standard legwear was usually replaced with black leather half-boots having coloured top edging and frontal tassel. Plumes, pompoms, cords and flounders of the shakos could be in many different colours (usually matching with that of the coat or with those of the trimming).

Drum-majors had the most ornate uniforms: these usually comprised a black bicorn trimmed with silver lace and having massive plumes (usually in the three colours of France's flag). They also had leather gauntlets and a laced baldric made of cloth to support their ornamental sabre. Their most important mark of distinction, however, was the corded mace that was used to direct the regimental band. In most cases the trimming of the drum-majors' uniforms was silver to match the epaulettes worn on the shoulders. As an alternative to the bicorn, these veteran musicians could have a busby made of fur similar to that worn by the contemporary French light cavalry. Drum-corporals were dressed like drum-majors, but with less decoration. The musicians of the single companies were dressed in a much simpler way and looked more or less like their comrades. They had coloured lacing on the facings, on the

Above left: **Carabinier of the light infantry in 1806.**

Above right: **Chasseur NCO of the light infantry wearing 1806 shako. (Photo and © Pascal Thonon)**

pockets and on the turn-backs. In addition, they usually had decorative stripes of coloured lace applied on the sleeves and coloured shoulder-wings. Their shako ornaments, company distinctions, badges on the turn-backs and epaulettes matched those of the ordinary soldiers.

1812 Bardin's Regulations

On 19 January 1812, new dress regulations came into being for the French infantry. These remained in use until the definitive fall of Napoleon in 1815, and were named after Major Bardin, who was responsible for their issue. They retained the general features and colours of the established dress but introduced some important modifications. The old coat was replaced with a double-breasted and short-tailed medium blue jacket known as *habit-veste*. It had plastron-style lapels on the front and vertical pockets on the

Uniforms of the light infantry carabiniers; from left to right: carabinier with 'busby' hat, carabiniers with bearskin, carabiniers with 1806 shako, and carabinier with 1812 uniform.

Uniforms of the light infantry; from left to right: sergeant-major of the voltigeurs, voltigeur with 'busby' hat, voltigeur with shako and chasseurs with shako.

back. The medium blue short turn-backs of the new uniform bore a white hunting horn for chasseurs, a red flaming grenade for carabiniers, and a yellow hunting horn for voltigeurs. Chasseurs had medium blue shoulder straps piped in white, while voltigeurs had yellow shoulder straps piped in medium blue, and carabiniers had red shoulder straps piped in medium blue. Rank distinctions and service chevrons remained unchanged. The medium blue waistcoat, which was no longer visible, now had a lower collar and the same shoulder straps as the coat. The black or white gaiters no longer extended over the knee.

The 1812 dress regulations introduced a new model of shako, with a new kind of white metal frontal plate that bore a crowned Imperial Eagle atop a semi-circular plate into which the regimental number was cut inside a hunting horn. The usual tricolour cockade and white metal chinscales of the previous model of shako were retained. Cords and flounders were officially abolished, but in practice they continued to be worn by most of the regiments. Carabiniers' shakos had red top and bottom bands as well as red side chevrons. Voltigeurs' shakos had yellow top and bottom bands as well as yellow side chevrons. The shakos of the chasseurs had tufted pompoms in company colour (green for 1st Company, sky blue for 2nd Company, orange for 3rd Company and violet for 4th Company), while those of the elite companies had tufted pompoms and plumes in red for carabiniers and in yellow for voltigeurs.

The Bardin Regulations introduced a new model of forage cap that replaced the previous bonnet de police; this was known as the *pokalem* and was a pie-shaped medium blue cap with a folding neck flap that could be fastened under the chin. The pokalem was piped with white and bore the regimental number or the grenadier/voltigeur badge embroidered in white on the front.

Chasseurs

The new uniform of a chasseur according to the 1812 dress regulations was: black shako with black top and bottom bands, white metal chinscales and frontal plate, national cockade and pompom in company colour; medium blue habit-veste with medium blue collar and pointed cuffs piped in white, medium blue shoulder straps piped in white, medium blue frontal plastron piped in white, white metal buttons, medium blue short turn-backs piped in white with embroidered company badge, medium blue vertical pocket flaps piped in white on the back of the jacket, medium blue trousers, black or white gaiters.

Carabiniers

Carabiniers had red plume, pompom, side-chevrons and top and bottom bands on the; voltigeurs were yellow. In addition, the collar of the voltigeurs' jackets was yellow with white piping. In breach of the new regulations, almost all the carabinier and voltigeur companies continued to wear their coloured epaulettes after 1812. The Bardin Regulations attempted to regularise the uniforms of the musicians by introducing a standard Imperial livery to be worn by all. It consisted of a dark green single-breasted jacket decorated with stripes of lace having alternate yellow and green segments. The yellow segments were decorated with an interwoven dark green crowned 'N', while the dark green segments were decorated with an interwoven yellow Imperial Eagle.

Drum-majors were to have double silver lace on the collar, while ordinary musicians had the decorative lace of the jacket on the collar and cuffs. Collar, cuffs and shoulder straps were green. Despite the new dress regulations, however, many bands continued to wear their previous regimental distinctions (such as busby hats) of which they were particularly fond. During the brief restoration of the Bourbons in 1814, some elements of the light infantry uniforms were modified: the tricolour cockade was replaced by the old white one and a new shako plate bearing the coat of arms of the royal family came into use.

EQUIPMENT

The standard equipment of the French light infantry did not change during 1799–1815. It consisted of the following basic elements: a knapsack made of calfskin carried on the back by means of buff leather shoulder straps. Its closing flap fastened

Sapper of the light infantry carabiniers, with axe and white leather apron.

Officers of the light infantry; from left to right: officer with shako, officers with 'busby' hat and officer with 1812 uniform.

with three buff leather straps and metal buckles. In addition, a black leather cartridge box constructed around a wooden block which had holes designed to receive cartridges. An external flap closed the box, and was decorated with a white metal badge featuring a flaming grenade for carabiniers and hunting horn for chasseurs/voltigeurs. Infantrymen had one whitened buff leather crossbelt from which the cartridge box was suspended; and one whitened buff leather crossbelt from which a bayonet scabbard was suspended. The cartridge box was worn on the right hip, the bayonet scabbard was worn on the left hip. The great coat was transported on top of the knapsack and was kept in position with three white leather straps fastened with metal buckles. The fatigue cap was attached to the bottom part of the cartridge box. The bayonet scabbard was made of black leather and had brass fittings.

Unlike the line infantry, all the companies of a light infantry battalion carried a short sword that was fastened alongside the bayonet scabbard. The short sword had a scabbard made of black leather with brass fittings. In addition to those described above, non-regulation pieces of equipment were also carried: these included canvas satchels of various dimensions and canteens. The latter ranged from wooden barrels to bottles having wicker-work cases; metal flasks suspended on coloured cord were quite popular. On campaign, especially in the Iberian Peninsula, dried pumpkins were often transformed into rudimentary canteens.

The standard weapon of the French chasseurs was the M1777 'Charleville' musket, a smoothbore flintlock of 17.5mm calibre with iron fittings. This was produced in a 141.7cm-long shortened version specifically designed for light infantry, having a weight of 4.375kg. The bayonet of the Charleville musket was 45.6cm long and triangular in section. The *sabre-briquet*, or short sword, had a cast-brass hilt and a curved guard ending in a pyramidal or rounded quillon. The blade of this weapon was curved like that of a cavalry sabre. The sword knot of the sabre-briquet was green for chasseurs, red for carabiniers and yellow for voltigeurs. Officers carried a straight-bladed sword with single-bar guard and helmet-shaped pommel, which was suspended on a shoulder belt or a waistbelt passing beneath the front flap of the breeches. The scabbard of this elegant weapon was made of black leather and had gilded metal fittings. The sword knots of officers were silver.

Chapter 3

Special Infantry Units

The French infantry was supported by a number of special units that performed specific duties and had a lot in common with the line or light regiments in terms of training as well as of uniforms.

Volontaires Bonaparte

After returning from his Egyptian Campaign, during the last months of 1799 Napoleon's Italian Army was in a deplorable condition. The Austrians and Russians had obtained a series of victories during his absence and all the territorial gains that France had achieved during 1796–97 had practically been lost. The Army of Italy had to be re-built since it had been almost destroyed in a series of engagements that were all extremely negative for France. To attract more volunteers and to have a corps of loyal supporters who could follow him on the battlefields of northern Italy and the Rhineland, on 8 March 1800, Napoleon authorised the creation of new volunteer corps to be formed by young enthusiasts coming from the middle classes of the Republic. Three such new units were formed, receiving the designation of Bonaparte's Volunteers or First Consul's Reserve Legion.

Of the three units, two were battalions of light infantry and one was a regiment of hussars. Most of the young men who had joined the ranks of Bonaparte's Volunteers wanted to serve as cavalrymen, but could not provide themselves with horses and thus had to serve as light infantrymen. The government provided them with elegant uniforms to keep morale high. Each of the two battalions of light infantry had nine companies, which were later assembled to form a temporary demi-brigade. The hussar regiment continued to act independently. In the early weeks of 1801, after little action, Bonaparte's Volunteers were disbanded and their members were absorbed into different regular units (those of the 1st Battalion were included in the 45th line half-brigade, those of the 2nd Battalion were included in the 17th light half-brigade).

The light infantry uniform of this corps was very elegant: it comprised a black Corsican hat and a light blue coat. The coat had a collar, pointed cuffs, front lapels, shoulder straps and turn-backs, all in yellow. The Corsican hat was adorned with a national cockade and with a light blue plume on the brim that was turned up on the left side. It was surmounted by a black crest and around it there was a wrapped band of light blue cloth. The uniform was completed by a white double-breasted waistcoat and trousers worn with black half-boots with piping at the top and a tassel at the front, both in white.

Garde Municipale de Paris

The capital of France had always had a special guard corps, acting both as garrison of the city and urban police and tasked with keeping order. In 1789, the Paris Guard sided with the revolutionaries and was retained in service by the new government. Two years later, however, it was disbanded following the general reorganisation of the *Gendarmerie* (France's militarised police). With the creation and the expansion of the National Guard, which had several units in Paris, the French capital did not require an independent corps of militarised police. This situation came to an end in 1802, when First Consul Napoleon created a strong corps of militarised policemen who could keep order in the capital. Until the proclamation of Empire, Paris was always on the verge of revolt and the masses were a potential menace for any ruling government. In addition, the French capital was the main base of all the royalist and foreign spies active in France.

Above left: **Officer of the Spanish Gendarmerie wearing** *bonnet de police* **fatigue cap. Inside his paramilitary Gendarmerie, Napoleon created an autonomous Spanish Gendarmerie that was specifically tasked with operating in French-occupied Spain. (Photo: Le Livre, l'Histoire et l'Obusier, © Rose-Hélène Ledanseur)**

Above right: **Trooper (left) and trumpeter (right) of the Municipal Guard of Paris cavalry.**

The new Municipal Guard of Paris came into existence on 4 October 1802. It consisted of two half-brigades (regiments from 1804) that were mostly recruited from old veterans of the French Army as well as from former members of the Gendarmerie. These men were experienced soldiers/policemen, having served for at least ten years and participated in at least five military campaigns. The 1st half-brigade was tasked with guarding all the entrances to the French capital, while the 2nd was tasked with garrisoning various areas of the vast city. Attached to the two infantry units was a squadron of dragoons, which patrolled the major streets and also acted as an honour guard, as required. Originally, the Municipal Guard of Paris was under the control of the city's civilian authorities. On 18 May 1806, it was transferred to the authority of the Ministry of War.

From an organisational point of view, the two infantry demi-brigades consisted of two battalions with five companies each, while the squadron of dragoons had two mounted companies. From 1805, the first battalion of each half-brigade was sent to serve with the army and participated in the military campaigns of 1805–07 as part of the French Army's reserves. During 1808–12, the composite demi-brigade of the

Municipal Guard serving with the army fought with great distinction in Spain, where its members could show all their valour as veteran soldiers. On 12 February 1812, the units that were stationed in Paris were reorganised as a single regiment of line infantry formed by two battalions. Each battalion had one company of grenadiers, one company of voltigeurs and four companies of fusiliers. On 23 October 1812, while Napoleon was in Russia, the Municipal Guard of Paris participated in a failed military coup organised against the Emperor by General Malet. This event marked the end of the corps. After the coup, Napoleon returned to Paris and disbanded the Municipal Guard. Its members were absorbed into the 134th Line Regiment.

The squadron of dragoons, which were not part of the coup, was absorbed into the Dutch Lancers of the Imperial Guard in February 1813. The two infantry regiments of the Municipal Guard of Paris were dressed with colourful uniforms and thus their members were commonly known as the *perroquets* or 'little parrots'. The 1st Regiment had a dark green uniform with red facings while the 2nd Regiment had a red uniform with dark green facings. All the general features of the dress were the same as that worn by the line infantry. In 1806, when several line regiments received the experimental white uniform, the Municipal Guard of Paris was included. The new uniform matched that introduced for the line regiments, being white with green facings for the 1st Regiment and white with red facings for the 2nd Regiment. This was retained in use until 1812.

Chasseurs de Montagne

Following his invasion of Spain in August 1808, Napoleon raised special battalions of light infantry from the French departments bordering the Iberian territories along the Pyrenees. For a long time, the French Army had included special corps of light skirmishers recruited from the mountains located on the frontier with Spain. These were made up of *miquelets*, ie, mountaineers who lived on the Pyrenees and who fought by using hit-and-run tactics. Since the French Army's lines of communication/supply crossed the Pyrenees, Napoleon chose to revive the traditions of the miquelets by organising units of mountain infantry that could patrol the frontier between France and Spain across the mountains. The main task of the new Chasseurs de Montagne was to protect the lines of communication/supply of the French Army from the attacks of Spanish insurgents or *guerrilleros*, who organised effective ambushes and were great skirmishers.

The new battalions of mountain infantry, five in total, were recruited from the Pyrenaic departments who opposed conscription because they did not wish to leave their home territories to serve in the army. These individuals frequently formed bands of brigands and survived by pillaging in the countryside; now they had the opportunity to serve in the army but remain in their home localities. To receive a pardon from the government for refusing conscription, many volunteers enlisted in the new battalions. The Battalion of the Eastern Pyrenees, the Battalion of the Upper Pyrenees, the Battalion of the Lower Pyrenees and the Battalion of Ariège each had eight companies, while the Battalion of Upper Garonne had two companies.

In the Lower Pyrenees and in Ariège, the local prefects had so many volunteers for the Chasseurs de Montagne that second battalions, each with eight companies, could be formed. Each mountain infantry company consisted of one captain, one lieutenant, one sub-lieutenant, one sergeant-major, four sergeants, one corporal-fourrier, eight corporals, one drummer and 130 privates. Soon after their formation, however, the battalions of Chasseurs de Montagne were sent to fight in Spain as light infantry and thus left their home departments. This was seen as a betrayal by most of the miquelets and many deserted soon after they were sent south.

On 17 January 1811, Napoleon was forced to reorganise his mountain infantry into just three battalions, numbered 1 to 3: the 1st Battalion comprised six companies coming from the Eastern

Carabinier of the Tirailleurs Corses in 1815. Note the peculiar Corsican hat worn as headgear.

Pyrenees, Upper Garonne and the Upper Pyrenees; the 2nd Battalion comprised eight companies coming from Ariège and the 3rd Battalion comprised eight companies coming from the Lower Pyrenees. In Spain, the Chasseurs de Montagne fought extremely well and were among the few French units that were able to counter the local guerrilleros. Following the French evacuation from Spain in 1814, the three battalions were absorbed into other units: the 1st Battalion into the 116th Line Regiment, the 2nd Battalion in the 4th Light Regiment and the 3rd Battalion in the 25th Light Regiment.

The Chasseurs de Montagne were dressed like the light infantry, but their uniform was entirely brown instead of medium blue; it had light blue facings and piping.

Tirailleurs Corses

Corsica, the home region of Napoleon, was annexed by France in 1770 after being under control of Genoa for several centuries. During the Revolution, the island revolted against the new republican government and was independent for a short period, supported by Britain's military. By 1797, however, the French had been able to re-occupy Corsica. On 8 July 1802, Napoleon chose to raise a light infantry battalion from the inhabitants of the large Mediterranean island. Corsicans were excellent hunters due to the mountainous terrain of their home territories. Initially, the light battalion recruited from Corsicans was a standard unit of chasseurs. It was included as the 3rd Battalion in the 8th Light Infantry Regiment but was administratively autonomous.

The unit consisted of nine active companies plus one depot company. In May 1804, the battalion was detached from its parent regiment and became a fully independent corps, assuming the new denomination of Tirailleurs Corses. During 1805–09, the Corsican light infantrymen participated in all the most important campaigns fought by the French Army and distinguished themselves on several occasions. Their battalion, at this point, had a standard establishment with six companies. On 8 September 1811, the Tirailleurs Corses were disbanded and absorbed into the newly raised 11th Light Regiment, of which they became the 1st Battalion.

In 1814, following Napoleon's first abdication, the restored monarchy decided to raise two new battalions of Tirailleurs Corses. When the Emperor returned in 1815, he transferred these two units to mainland France to fight the Allies and organised another two battalions that would have remained in Corsica. Following the second abdication of Napoleon, all four battalions of Tirailleurs Corses were disbanded.

Until 1804, the Corsican light infantrymen were dressed exactly like the standard chasseurs, but with facings and piping in green on their medium blue uniforms. They also had green cords and flounders on their shako. In 1804, they received a distinctive uniform, which had the same cut and main features as that worn by the standard light infantrymen, but it was entirely brown. The facings and piping remained green on this new uniform, to match the cords and flounders of the shako. Around 1808, the dress of the Tirailleurs Corses was partly modified: the cuffs became pointed and the frontal lapels formed a single plastron mirroring the coats introduced by the Bardin Regulations. From this point forwards, the collar, cuffs and frontal plastron became all red.

The re-formed Tirailleurs Corses of 1815 received a new uniform that included a black Corsican hat with the left brim turned up. The brim featured a national cockade and a pompom in company colour. The coat, always brown, was of the new model introduced in 1812 for all the French foot troops; it had collar, pointed cuffs and piping in green. The trousers, which had been brown until 1811, were now green. The personal equipment used by the Tirailleurs Corses matched that of the light infantry chasseurs, but included a peculiar ammunition *carchera*, or pouch, that was carried on the belly. All the belt equipment, including a single crossbelt for the bayonet and short sword, was in buff leather.

In addition to the Tirailleurs Corses, during 1803–05, the French Army comprised five battalions of Corsican light infantry that were stationed on their home island in order to counter local bandits or insurgents who resented French rule. Each of these territorial battalions of light infantry comprised one company of carabiniers and four companies of chasseurs. In 1806, when Corsica was fully pacified, Napoleon transferred the five units to Italy. At that time, the French Army was conquering the Kingdom of Naples. Before leaving Corsica, the five battalions were assembled into a single corps known as the Corsican Legion; once in Italy, all the carabinier companies of the new unit assembled to form an elite carabinier battalion. After the French completed their conquest of the Kingdom of Naples, the Corsican Legion was transferred to the new Neapolitan Army that was to serve Joseph Bonaparte (the new King of Naples). In November 1806, the Corsican Legion received the new designation of Corsican Light Regiment and was reorganised into three battalions with nine companies each (one of carabiniers and eight of chasseurs). It remained part of the Neapolitan Army until 1813. The light infantrymen of the Corsican Legion were dressed exactly like the French chasseurs, but the collar of their coat was green.

Chapter 4

Foreign Units

Since the days of Louis XIV, in the last quarter of the 17th century, the French Army had always included a sizeable number of foreign regiments; some of these, like the Swiss ones, had an excellent military reputation and were in the service of France from the 15th century. During the Revolution, many foreign volunteers went to France to fight under the flags of the new Republic and soon became an important component of the French military forces. Napoleon, after becoming First Consul in 1799, continued the traditional French policy of including substantial numbers of foreigners in the military forces and sponsored the formation of several new corps made up of non-French soldiers.

Swiss Regiments

Following the fall of the monarchy in 1792, all foreign military units were disbanded. Swiss soldiers were the last defenders of the French royal family and were particularly hated by the rebels. In 1798, France invaded Switzerland as part of its revolutionary expansion and transformed the country into a puppet state known as the Helvetian Republic. Once in control of Switzerland, the French government asked the political representatives of the Helvetian Republic to raise six demi-brigades of line infantry to serve with the French Army. During 1799, however, Switzerland was invaded by the Allies and became – for several months – the battlefield of the ongoing military confrontation between France and the Austro-Russians.

In the early months of 1800, after the Helvetian Republic returned to French control, Napoleon could reorganise the Swiss military forces. The First Consul was never particularly loved by the Swiss, since he wanted to transform the Helvetian Republic into a centralised state by abolishing its traditional administrative organisation based on cantons. The Swiss guarded their cantonal autonomy and opposed Napoleon's proposed reforms in every possible way.

The First Consul wanted to create an autonomous Swiss Army that would have been under the control of the Helvetian Republic (and known as the Helvetian Legion) as well as four Swiss half-brigades that would have been part of the French Army. After long discussions with the Swiss authorities, Napoleon accepted a compromise in 1802. The Helvetian Legion was disbanded and the old canton militias were reformed. At the same time, however, the Swiss agreed to provide 16,000 soldiers to the French Army, organised into four line-infantry regiments. The new regiments were recruited during 1805–07. However, during 1799–1805, three under-strength Swiss demi-brigades served with the French Army instead of the four that had been required in 1798.

The four Swiss regiments raised during 1805–07 soon proved to be excellent units. They were well regarded for their valour and participated in all the most important military campaigns fought by the French Army during 1808–14. Each of the four regiments comprised four active battalions plus an independent company of artillery; a single battalion consisted of one grenadier company, one voltigeur company and seven fusilier companies. The regimental staff and the single companies had the same internal organisation as the standard French ones. The artillery company had four officers and 64 gunners who served two 4-pounder guns.

In March 1812, after several years of service in Spain and after the Swiss Confederation signed a new capitulation with France, the four infantry regiments were reorganised. Each was to have three active battalions instead of four, plus one depot half-battalion. The single artillery company in each regiment was retained, but it was re-equipped with two 3-pounder guns. The new active battalions were smaller than the previous ones, since each comprised one grenadier company, one voltigeur company and four fusilier companies. A year after the disastrous Russian campaign of 1812, in which all Swiss regiments participated, the regiments were re-organised as single-battalion regiments due to the heavy losses suffered. Following the restoration of the French royal family in 1814, the four Swiss regiments returned home. In 1815, Napoleon tried to organise a new Swiss infantry regiment structured on two battalions with Swiss soldiers loyal to him, but ultimately only one battalion participated in the Belgian campaign that culminated with the Battle of Waterloo.

The three Swiss half-brigades of 1799–1805 were dressed in red, the traditional colour of the Swiss regiments in French service. Their uniforms matched the French line infantry, but in red and with distinctive colours for facings and piping. The 1st demi-brigade had white facings and dark blue piping; the 2nd demi-brigade had dark blue facings and white piping; the 3rd demi-brigade had yellow facings and sky-blue piping. The trousers and waistcoats were dark blue until 1800, when they were replaced with white ones. During 1805–07, the

Grenadier (left) and voltigeur (right) of the 3rd Swiss Regiment. Note the peculiar brass plate of the bearskin.

four new regiments continued to be dressed like the French line infantry but in red: the 1st Regiment had yellow facings and dark blue piping; the 2nd Regiment had dark blue facings and yellow piping; the 3rd Regiment had black facings and white piping; the 4th Regiment had sky-blue facings and white piping.

The grenadiers of the Swiss regiments wore a peculiar bearskin with a brass frontal plate that bore an Imperial Eagle. The musicians wore uniforms in the piping colour of their regiment instead of red ones. In 1812, with the introduction of the Bardin Regulations, the colours of facings and piping were modified as follows: the 1st Regiment had yellow facings and yellow piping; the 2nd Regiment had dark blue facings and red piping; the 3rd Regiment had black facings and red piping; the 4th Regiment had sky-blue facings and red piping. In addition to the four Swiss regiments, the French Army also included two independent battalions of Swiss infantry that were provided by two semi-autonomous areas of Switzerland: the Canton of Valais and the Principality of Neuchatel (neither were part of the Swiss Confederation and are covered separately.

Valais Battalion

The Canton of Valais, located in south-west Switzerland, included the strategically fundamental Alpine passes of Simplon and Great Saint Bernard. For this reason, Napoleon supported those political exponents of the canton who wanted to secede from the Swiss Confederation. In 1802, the Canton of Valais became independent under the protection of France, then, in October 1805, Valais agreed to recruit a battalion of line infantry to serve with the French Army. The new unit had a small establishment with one grenadier company and four fusilier companies. Like all the other Swiss cantons, in addition to this battalion recruited for French service, Valais had an autonomous home-defence militia.

Like the four Swiss regiments, the Valais Battalion was sent to Spain, where it fought with great distinction and suffered heavy losses. On 12 November 1810, Napoleon annexed the Canton of Valais to France; some months later, in 1811, the Valais Battalion was incorporated into the new 11th Light Infantry of the French Army.

The soldiers of the Valais Battalion were dressed like the French line infantry but wore red coats with white facings and red piping. The grenadier company of the unit did not have bearskins but wore shakos with red company distinctions.

Neuchatel Battalion

In 1806, the small Principality of Neuchatel, located in north-west Switzerland, was ceded to France by Prussia. Instead of annexing the small state to France, Napoleon gave it to his Chief-of-Staff, Marshal Berthier (who became Prince of Neuchatel). On 11 May 1807, the military forces of the Principality of

Above left: **NCO of the Swiss infantry wearing bonnet de police fatigue cap. (Photo and © Pascal Thonon)**

Above middle: **Sapper of the 3rd Swiss Regiment; note the long beard and the peculiar badges embroidered on the sleeves.**

Above right: **Gunner of the Neuchatel Battalion's artillery.**

Neuchatel were organised as a single line infantry battalion with six companies: one of grenadiers, one of voltigeurs and four of fusiliers (each with 160 men). Attached to the battalion was a mixed company of artillery and engineers consisting of four officers, 14 NCOs, 32 gunners, 16 train drivers and 16 sappers. The company was equipped with two 6-pounder guns.

The Neuchatel Battalion served with distinction on several occasions, especially in Spain, until being officially disbanded in June 1814. The soldiers of the Neuchatel Battalion were known as 'canaries' because of their yellow uniforms. In fact, they were dressed like the French line infantry but with yellow coats having red facings.

Italian Legion

In the spring of 1799, the Cisalpine Republic, in northern Italy, the largest of France's puppet states, created by Napoleon during 1797, was temporarily invaded by Austro-Russian military forces. The Cisalpine Army, which was numerically large, was disbanded following the fall of the republic but many of its members remained loyal to Napoleon and followed the French during their retreat. As a result, the First Consul created an Italian Legion inside the French Army, made up of former Cisalpine soldiers. The new unit, formed on 8 September 1799, comprised four battalions of line infantry and four squadrons of mounted chasseurs as well as one company of light artillery.

Each of the infantry battalions had one company of grenadiers, one company of chasseurs and eight companies of fusiliers. In January 1800, another two battalions were added to the Italian Legion, but the latter was disbanded a few weeks later when the Cisalpine Republic was restored following the Battle of Marengo.

The infantry of the Italian Legion was dressed like the contemporary French light infantry, but in medium green instead of medium blue and with yellow facings/piping.

In addition to the Italian Legion, the French Army of 1799–1800 included an independent Italian Battalion of line infantry made up of Italian political refugees. This battalion was dressed in similar fashion to French line infantry but with collar and cuffs of the coat in green.

Tirailleurs du Po

In March 1801, the Duchy of Parma, one of the many small states of the Italian peninsula, was annexed by France and its army disbanded. In April 1803, Napoleon raised a light infantry unit from the new Italian departments that had been organised on the territories of the former Duchy of Parma. This new corps, a battalion, assumed the denomination Tirailleurs du Po since most of its members came from the areas located on the banks of the Po River. The battalion consisted of one carabinier company and five chasseur companies. From 1805, it served with distinction as part of the French Army fighting at Austerlitz, Jena, Eylau and Friedland. The Italian soldiers from this battalion were considered among the best light infantry of the French Army and were particularly admired by Napoleon. In 1811, the battalion ceased to be an independent unit when it was absorbed into the new 11th Light Regiment of the French Army (becoming the 2nd Battalion).

The Tirailleurs du Po were dressed like the contemporary French light infantry, but retained the bicorn (with falling plume) as their headgear until 1811. In addition, their coats had a collar, pointed cuffs, front lapels and turn-backs in red with white piping.

Piedmontese Legion

in 1799 what remained of the Piedmontese Army was absorbed into the French Army, since Piedmont (officially known as the Kingdom of Sardinia) was annexed to France. The Piedmontese soldiers were re-organised into two demi-brigades of line infantry, one of light infantry, one regiment of dragoons and one regiment of mounted chasseurs. These units were soon disbanded and none was in existence by 1803.

The Piedmontese Army of pre-1799 included five line-infantry regiments of Swiss mercenaries. The French tried to retain these experienced soldiers in their service by reorganising them into two legions, but those legions did not last. As a result, on 18 May 1803, Napoleon ordered the formation of four legions made up of former Piedmontese soldiers to be recruited from the Italian departments of the French Republic.

- Each legion was to comprise three battalions of line infantry, two battalions of light infantry and one company of artillery.
- The single battalions consisted of one elite company of grenadiers/carabiniers and four companies of fusiliers/chasseurs.

Ultimately, only one of the four planned legions could be formed and it became known as Piedmontese Legion or Légion du Midi. It served in Haiti before being reduced, in 1808, to a single battalion of light infantry (with one company of carabiniers, one company of voltigeurs and three companies of chasseurs). The unit was then sent to Spain.

Meanwhile, Napoleon organised a new Piedmontese battalion that became known as 2nd Piedmontese Legion, but this did not last long either. In 1811, the 1st Piedmontese Legion was disbanded.

During its history, the Piedmontese Legion used two different uniforms; the first, worn for just a few months during 1803, was like that of the French line infantry but in grey with red facings/piping and incorporating the light infantry shako as headgear. The grey was soon replaced with dark brown and the fusilier companies replaced their shako with a very specific helmet (similar to that worn by the French dragoons) made of black leather, with brass frontal plate and brass crest, and a tufted pompom on the front of the crest in company colour. The facings and piping of the new uniform were light blue. The black helmet was retained in use until 1808, when it was replaced by the standard line infantry shako.

Hanoverian Legion

In 1803, following the French occupation of Hanover, a German state governed by the same royal family that ruled Great Britain, Napoleon organised a legion made up of former members of the recently disbanded Hanoverian Army who wanted to serve under his flags. This new Hanoverian Legion was to consist of one light infantry regiment (with two battalions) and one regiment of mounted chasseurs (with four squadrons). Desertion and sickness, however, prevented the new corps from reaching its planned establishment. The unit served in Spain, where it performed auxiliary functions.

On 10 March 1810, the Westphalian Battalion (another foreign unit) was absorbed into the Hanoverian Legion, enabling two battalions to be formed. On 11 August 1811, however, the corps was disbanded after having suffered severe losses in Spain.

The infantry of the Hanoverian Legion was dressed like the French line infantry, but with red coats with dark blue facings/piping. The coats for the new corps were initially produced from the stores of cloth found in the magazines of the Hanoverian Army (which was dressed in red like the British Army).

La Tour d'Auvergne Regiment

This unit was created in September 1805 and was made up of POWs captured during the campaign fought against the Austrians and Russians that year. The name of the corps, which was mostly made up of German-speaking soldiers, derived from its commander who was the Prince of La Tour d'Auvergne. It consisted of three light infantry battalions with six companies each (one of carabiniers, one of voltigeurs and four of chasseurs). In 1809, with the new Austrian POWs captured at Wagram, a fourth battalion was added to the regiment. Two years later, in 1811, another two battalions made up of Spanish/Portuguese POWs were added to the unit. In that same year, the corps assumed the new denomination of 1st Foreign Regiment. After being reduced to just four battalions, it was disbanded in the last weeks of 1813.

The soldiers of La Tour d'Auvergne Regiment were dressed like the French light infantrymen, but entirely in dark green instead of medium blue; in addition, the collar and cuff flaps of their coats were red.

Isembourg Regiment

This unit was created in November 1805 and was made up of POWs captured during the campaign fought against the Austro-Russians that year. The name of the corps, which was mostly made up of German-speaking soldiers, derived from its commander who was the Prince of Isembourg. It consisted of four light infantry battalions with nine companies each (one of carabiniers, one of voltigeurs and seven of chasseurs). The Isembourg Regiment became a sort of foreign legion, from 1809 when it started to incorporate an increasing number of Spanish and Portuguese POWs. On 16 October 1810, the unit was reorganised as six battalions, each comprising six companies. On 3 August 1811, it was renamed as the 2nd Foreign Regiment of the French Army. A few days after receiving the new denomination, the Isembourg Regiment absorbed what remained of the disbanded Hanoverian Legion. The corps ceased to exist in 1814, like most of the other foreign units of the French Army.

The soldiers of the Isembourg Regiment were dressed like the French light infantrymen, but with yellow collar and cuff flaps on their coats.

Prussian Regiment

Following the defeat of Prussia at Jena and Auerstadt on 13 November 1806, Napoleon raised a new infantry regiment from the many Prussian POWs in French hands. The new unit, simply known as the Prussian Regiment, was structured on three battalions. The first of these served in Spain, while the other two fought against the British in the Netherlands during 1809. The Prussian Regiment, however, frequently suffered from high desertion rates and was never an elite unit. In 1810, its battalions were reduced from three to two, and in 1811, the unit became the new 4th Foreign Regiment of the French Army. After being sent to Spain and performing poorly, the Prussian Regiment was deployed as a

Above left: **Chasseur of the Hanoverian Legion.**

Above right: **Trooper of the Hanoverian Legion's cavalry.**

Uniforms of La Tour d'Auvergne Regiment; from left to right: hornist of the voltigeurs, carabinier and chasseur.

garrison unit in the Netherlands before rebelling against French authorities on 19 November 1813. A few days after these events, it was officially disbanded.

The Prussian Regiment uniform was like that of the French light infantry. Its coat and trousers were dark green, the former having red facings/piping. The coat lapels formed a single plastron prior to the introduction of the 1812 dress regulations.

Chasseurs of the Isembourg Regiment.

Westphalia Regiment

On 11 December 1806, Napoleon decreed the formation of a new foreign regiment made up of Prussian POWs captured during the 1806 campaign. It consisted of four line-infantry battalions, each with six companies (one of grenadiers, one of voltigeurs and four of fusiliers). By June 1807, however, most of the unit's original soldiers had deserted and the regiment was restructured as two battalions. In November 1807, the 1st Battalion was sent to Spain, where it was later absorbed into the Hanoverian Legion. As a result, the remaining 2nd Battalion started to be known as the Westphalia Battalion. It existed until

1813, when its members were absorbed into the army of the Kingdom of Westphalia, a puppet state of France.

The soldiers of the Westphalia Regiment were dressed like French line infantrymen, but their coats were white with red facings/piping.

Irish Legion

Following the Irish Rebellion of 1798, a number of Irish insurgents fled to France as political exiles. The Irish formed quite a large community and from them, Napoleon organised a small Irish Legion and returned it to Ireland alongside other military units, to support local insurgents rebelling against the British government. This first unit, however, had a very small establishment and was extremely short-lived.

By 31 August 1803, as part of Napoleon's planned invasion of Great Britain, a new Irish Legion was raised from the Irish refugees living in France. This Irish Legion had a longer history than the first. Initially it consisted of a single battalion but was later expanded to become a regiment.

The Irish soldiers were the only foreigners of the French Army to receive an Imperial Eagle as their standard and were mostly stationed along the coast of northern France to perform garrison duties. From 1808, however, two battalions were sent to Spain, where they distinguished themselves on several occasions. In October 1810, the two battalions formed a single unit; returning to France in 1811, and at that point the whole Irish Legion received the new designation of 3rd Foreign Regiment. Napoleon chose to reorganise some of his most important foreign units, numbering them from 1 to 4.

During 1813–14, the 3rd Foreign Regiment fought with great distinction in Germany, suffering heavy casualties; following the first restoration of the French royal family, on 28 September 1814, the two battalions of the unit were disbanded.

The soldiers of the Irish Legion were always dressed like the French line infantrymen, but their coats were green (the Irish national colour) with yellow facings and piping.

Portuguese Legion

In 1807, the French Army occupied Portugal when that country refused to close its ports to the British military and merchant ships. The existing Portuguese Army was disbanded, and then reorganised as a 9,000-strong Portuguese Legion that would be part of the French Army. The new corps was organised on 12 November and initially comprised five regiments of line infantry, one battalion of light infantry, three regiments of mounted chasseurs, one battery of artillery, one depot battalion of infantry and one depot squadron of cavalry. It didn't take long before Portuguese soldiers deserted *en masse* on their journey from Spain to France and, as a result, the Portuguese Legion was reduced to three regiments of line infantry, one regiment of mounted chasseurs and one depot battalion.

The corps served with distinction in the Austrian campaign of 1809 and later took part in the Russian campaign of 1812. On Russian soil, the Portuguese soldiers fought with great determination, winning Napoleon's admiration. In 1813, after returning to France, the Portuguese Legion was reduced to just two battalions of infantry (one active and one depot). Both were disbanded on 5 May 1814, following the first abdication of Napoleon.

The infantrymen of the Portuguese Legion were dressed in a distinctive brown uniform that was very dark; for this reason they were commonly known as the Black Infantry. Their dress included a black shako with a crown that sloped down at the back in order to produce a 'false front', brass chinscales, brass frontal plate bearing unit number, black visor, brass unit badge (worn only by elite companies, and featuring a flaming grenade for grenadiers and a hunting horn for chasseurs), cords and flounders in company colour (worn only by elite companies, in red for grenadiers and in green for chasseurs) and plume (red tipped in yellow for fusiliers, red for grenadiers and green for chasseurs). In addition, they wore a dark brown coat with collar, round cuffs and frontal plastron in red with white piping. It featured white short turn-backs with red piping, dark brown shoulder straps piped in red for fusiliers (replaced by red epaulettes for grenadiers and by green epaulettes with red crescent for chasseurs). Dark brown trousers with red side stripe, white spats and black shoes completed the uniform. During summer, white trousers were worn loose and decorated with three red stripes on each side as well as with red decorative knots on the front.

Joseph Napoleon's Regiment

Until 1807, Spain was a loyal ally of Napoleon and fought with the French against the Allies. The Spanish monarchy sent an expeditionary force, made up of the best units of the Spanish Army, to the Baltic area in order to support the French Army operating there. This expeditionary force, known as the Division of the North, comprised four regiments of line infantry and two battalions of light infantry, among other units. When Napoleon invaded Spain and forced the ruling king to abdicate, most Spanish soldiers stationed on the Baltic refused to continue serving with the French. The Emperor proclaimed his brother, Joseph Bonaparte, to be King of Spain and was determined to annex the whole Iberian Peninsula to his Empire.

Against all odds, the Division of the North was evacuated from the Baltic with the support of the Royal Navy and returned to Spain to oppose the French invaders. However, before the evacuation could be completed, two Spanish line infantry regiments were surrounded and disarmed by the French.

During autumn 1808, Napoleon raised a new military unit from the Spanish POWs captured in the Baltic and as a result, on 13 February 1809, Joseph Napoleon's Regiment came into existence. It consisted of four active battalions and one depot battalion.

Each active battalion had four companies of fusiliers, one company of grenadiers and one company of voltigeurs. The new unit was never particularly loyal to the French and so was never sent to Spain. Joseph Bonaparte wanted to include it in his newly organised Spanish Army, but this was not possible. The regiment participated in the Russian campaign of 1812 and the German one of 1813, before being reduced to two battalions by mid-1813. On 25 November 1813, the unit was officially disbanded.

The soldiers of Joseph Bonaparte's Regiment were dressed like the French line infantrymen but with white coats having green facings and piping.

Polish Legions

The Poles were among the most numerous and loyal foreign soldiers of Napoleon's army during the whole period taken into account. They fought under the flags of the French Republic and later of the French Empire, with the objective of freeing their homeland from the foreign troops occupying it. In 1795, the Commonwealth of Poland and Lithuania had disappeared from the geographical maps of Europe when it was partitioned between three great powers: Austria, Prussia and Russia. Russia was hated by the Polish population, a nation that was at war with Revolutionary France; as a result, Poland and France had several enemies in common. After a last Polish national uprising was crushed in 1794, thousands of Polish patriots who had fought for the freedom of their country left their homeland as political refugees and went to France. Here they were organised into a Polish Legion that was to fight alongside the French, but since the new constitution of the French Republic did not allow the presence of foreign units inside the French Army, the Polish Legion was transferred to the recently organised Cisalpine Army of northern Italy. The Polish soldiers fought extremely well on several occasions and were admired by Napoleon. Thanks to their success and to the arrival of hundreds of new volunteers, a 2nd Polish Legion could be organised (which was always part of the Cisalpine Army). During 1799, the Poles suffered great losses in Italy, since the Allies organised an effective counter-offensive while Napoleon was in Egypt. The 2nd Legion was completely destroyed and ceased to exist; the 1st Legion was greatly reduced in numbers. With the temporary fall of the Cisalpine Republic, Napoleon decreed after his return to France that foreign troops could now serve as part of the French Army; as a result, the survivors of the 1st Polish Legion were reorganised as part of the Italian Legion and a new Danube Legion could be formed on the Rhine by recruiting new Polish volunteers (mostly POWs coming from the Austrian Army).

Danube Legion

This was the first Polish military unit of the French Army; it consisted of four line-infantry battalions, four squadrons of lancers and one company of mounted artillery. The corps served on the Rhine and later fought at the Battle of Marengo. In December 1801, the 1st Polish Legion and the Danube Legion were assembled and reorganised as three demi-brigades of infantry: the 1st, 2nd and 3rd Polish half-brigades. The first two were made up of former members of the 1st Polish

Uniforms of the Prussian Regiment; from left to right: musicians, officer and privates.

Legion, while the third was made up of former members of the Danube Legion. The 2nd Polish demi-brigade and the 3rd Polish demi-brigade were sent to Haiti by Napoleon in 1802, where they were annihilated by the local rebels and by yellow fever. In 1805, the 1st Polish half-brigade was re-named 1st Polish Legion and was assigned to the army of the Kingdom of Italy (the direct heir of the Cisalpine Republic). In 1806, the Polish Legion, now consisting of just one line infantry regiment and one lancer regiment, was transferred to the army of the Kingdom of Naples (recently conquered by the French). After a few months in southern Italy, however, the corps was disbanded.

Northern Legion

In 1807, during the war against Russia, Napoleon decided to raise a new Polish Legion from the many Polish POWs who had previously served in the Prussian Army. This unit was known as the Northern Legion and was to consist of two sub-legions with four infantry battalions each. Ultimately, only the first sub-legion came into existence. It served with distinction until 1808, when it was absorbed into the army of the newly constituted Grand Duchy of Warsaw. After great sacrifices, during 1807–08 the Poles fighting for Napoleon finally achieved their main objective: the creation of a new and independent Polish state in their homeland.

Legion of the Vistula

Before the birth of the Grand Duchy of Warsaw, which was a protectorate of the French Empire, Napoleon raised a second and larger Polish legion to be part of the French Army. He assembled the former members of the Polish Legion once in Neapolitan service with new volunteers and – in February 1807 – was able to organise a new Legion of the Vistula that comprised three regiments of line infantry and one regiment of lancers. After having been included among the units of the French Army on 21 February 1808, two of its infantry regiments participated in the invasion of Spain, together with the lancer regiment; the lancers were disbanded in 1811 and were absorbed into a newly organised French cavalry regiment. In Spain, the Polish soldiers distinguished themselves on several occasions.

2nd Vistula Legion

In 1809, after having defeated the Austrians at the Battle of Wagram, the Emperor decreed the formation of a 2nd Vistula Legion, with recruits from the Polish POWs who were previously in the Austrian Army. This new unit consisted of two infantry battalions and was disbanded in February 1810. Its members were transferred to the 4th Infantry Regiment of the 1st Vistula Legion. In 1812, in view of the Russian Campaign, the number of battalions in each infantry regiment of the Vistula Legion was increased from two to three. In addition, a small battery with two 3-pounder guns was attached to each infantry regiment. Of the 7,000 Polish soldiers who followed Napoleon into Russia at the beginning of the campaign, only 1,500 returned; as a result, on 18 June 1813, the Vistula Legion was reorganised as the single Vistula Regiment (having two battalions). With the restoration of the French royal family in 1814, the Vistula Regiment was disbanded.

Danube Legion Uniforms

The uniform of the Danube Legion infantry matched that of the French line infantry, while the lancers and the mounted artillery of the same corps had Polish-style uniforms. The three Polish demi-brigades, organised in 1801, were dressed in a distinctive national style with czapka headgear with a squared top, and 'kurtka' tunic with very short turn-backs and front lapels that formed a single plastron.

The uniform incorporated dark blue czapka with white edging to the outer seams, black bottom band and visor, national cockade, white metal badge (a Polish cross for fusiliers, a flaming grenade for grenadiers, a hunting horn for chasseurs), plume in company colour (white for fusiliers, red for grenadiers and green for chasseurs), cords and flounders in company colour. The dark blue kurtka with collar had round cuffs, frontal plastron and short turn-backs in regimental colour, dark blue trousers, black leather half-boots with top piping and frontal tassel in company colour. Fusiliers had dark blue shoulder straps piped in regimental colour, grenadiers had red epaulettes and chasseurs had green epaulettes. The regimental colour of the 1st Polish demi-brigade, which remained in Italy, was red. That of the 2nd Polish demi-brigade was yellow and that of the 3rd Polish demi-brigade was red.

The soldiers of the two latter units, after arriving in Haiti, replaced their czapka headgear

Grenadier of the Irish Legion.

with a more practical round hat made of straw. It should be noted that the battalions of the Polish half-brigades included one company of fusiliers less than their French equivalents but had one company of chasseurs each.

Northern Legion Uniforms

The infantry of the Northern Legion was dressed similarly to the demi-brigades of the previous years: black czapka with white edging to the outer seams, black bottom band and visor, national cockade, brass frontal plate bearing an Imperial Eagle, pompom and plume in company colour (light blue for fusiliers, red for grenadiers and yellow for voltigeurs), cords and flounders in company colour (white for fusiliers, red for grenadiers and yellow for voltigeurs). The dark blue kurtka with round cuffs, cuff flaps, frontal plastron and short turn-backs in red, dark blue collar piped in red, dark blue trousers with red side stripe and black gaiters.

Fusiliers had light blue epaulettes, grenadiers had red epaulettes and voltigeurs had yellow epaulettes.

Vistula Legion Uniforms

The infantry of the Vistula Legion was dressed with the following: black czapka with white edging to the outer seams, black bottom band and visor, national cockade, brass frontal plate bearing an Imperial Eagle, pompom in company colour (light blue for fusiliers, red for grenadiers and yellow for voltigeurs), cords and flounders in company colour (white for fusiliers, red for grenadiers and yellow for voltigeurs). The dark blue kurtka had collar, pointed cuffs, frontal plastron and short turn-backs in yellow; white trousers and black gaiters completed the outfit. Fusiliers had white epaulettes, grenadiers had red epaulettes and voltigeurs had yellow epaulettes. The czapka was later replaced by an ordinary shako, like that worn by the French line infantry.

Balkan Troops

During the Napoleonic Period, the French occupied, albeit for short periods, several areas of the Balkans and recruited a good number of military units from this area. During the period 1797–1815, the French controlled the Ionian Islands (also known as Seven Islands (1797–99 and 1807–14); Dalmatia and Istria (which were annexed to the Kingdom of Italy between 1805–09, and then to the French Empire between 1809–14); and the Illyrian Provinces (which were part of the French Empire between 1809–14). The Ionian Islands were part of the Republic of Venice's territories before 1797; when the Venetian state was ceded by Napoleon to Austria with the Treaty of Campoformio, they were annexed by France.

Great Britain and Russia were particularly interested in the conquest of the Ionian Islands and possession was particularly contested during the Napoleonic Period until the French reoccupied them in 1807. Dalmatia and Istria were obtained by Napoleon in 1805, following the Austrian defeat at Austerlitz. Until 1809, they were part of the Kingdom of Italy (a semi-independent state ruled by Napoleon) but were later annexed to the new Illyrian Provinces on their creation. Following the Austrian defeat of 1809 at Wagram, the French obtained more territories along the Illyrian coast and thus the Austrians lost their access to the Adriatic Sea. With the incorporation of new territories, Napoleon could add to the Illyrian Provinces the small Republic of Ragusa, which had been occupied by the French in 1806. The new Balkan provinces of the Empire were divided into six districts and had a very large population; they were invaded during the last months of 1813 by the Austrians with the decisive support of the Royal Navy.

Albanian Regiment

On 12 December 1807, after having re-conquered the Ionian Islands, the French raised an Albanian Regiment from the large Albanian community living on the archipelago. Since many Albanians from the Balkan mainland abandoned their homeland to re-settle as free farmers on the Ionian Islands, it was not difficult for the French to find enough recruits for the new unit. This consisted of three light infantry battalions, each with nine companies.

Greek Foot Chasseurs

On 10 March 1808, the French authorities recruited a new military corps in the Ionian Islands, this time from the Greek community that lived there. It was known as the Greek Foot Chasseurs and consisted of a single battalion with eight light infantry companies. In July 1809, the new unit was absorbed into the Albanian Regiment, which was restructured as six battalions with six companies each. On 6 November 1813, after the British captured some of the Ionian Islands, the Albanian Regiment was reduced to just two battalions and was officially disbanded in June 1814.

The soldiers of both the Albanian Regiment and the Greek Foot Chasseurs never received regular uniforms; they were dressed in national costume, which included a tunic with short skirt or *tunique fustanella*, worn under a short scarlet vest with sleeves open to the elbow and a thick goatskin cloak.

Uniforms of the Portuguese Legion's infantry (left) and cavalry (right).

Septinsular Battalion

In addition to the corps described above, the French raised another military unit from the Ionian Islands: the so-called Septinsular Battalion, a light infantry battalion with six companies. It was made up of soldiers who had previously formed the Venetian garrison of the Ionian Islands. In 1808, it was expanded to nine companies, but since it performed quite badly against the British, the corps was disbanded in 1812.

The soldiers of the Septinsular Battalion were dressed exactly like the French light infantry, but with light blue facings and piping (including the side stripe of trousers).

Oriental Chasseurs

During his Egyptian campaign of 1798–99, Napoleon recruited large numbers of Greeks, Copts, Turks and Syrians as auxiliaries. When the French left Egypt in 1801, several of these soldiers went to France, where they were reorganised as a light infantry battalion with eight companies (later increased to ten), known as the Oriental Chasseurs. This unit served with distinction and was later attached to the Albanian Regiment of the Ionian Islands in 1809. It participated in several campaigns on mainland Europe until being disbanded on 24 September 1814. The Oriental Chasseurs were dressed like a standard light infantry battalion of the French Army.

Illyrian Military Units

After Napoleon annexed the whole of Illyria to his Empire in 1809, the French inherited six regiments of 'Grenz' (frontier) infantry from the Austrian Empire. To protect their Illyrian territories from the incursions of the Ottomans, in fact, the Austrians raised six regiments of light infantry from the warlike communities along the Balkan coastline. The frontier soldiers of Illyria lived in military settlements that were located along the border with the Ottoman Empire and were organised according to the 'zadruga' system (which was based on extended family homesteads).

Most of the frontier soldiers were Croats, but there were also significant numbers of Christian refugees coming from Bosnia. They were extremely loyal to the Austrian government, since they received their farms in exchange for military service. The 'Grenzers' were famous for their tactical skills as light infantry skirmishers and were used to fight on mountain terrain.

Croatian Regiments

With the French occupation of Illyria, Napoleon had a total of 16,000 frontier soldiers under his command; these had been released from their oath of allegiance to the Austrian Empire and could now serve as part of the French Army. They were reorganised as six regiments of **Illyrian Chasseurs**, which were also known as Croatian Regiments; the original Austrian internal composition of the units was retained and thus each regiment was to comprise two active battalions (with six light companies each) plus a depot with two companies. In case of war, the number of active battalions was increased to four, since the two depot companies could be enlarged to become battalions. In 1812, the internal establishment of the regiments of Illyrian Chasseurs was increased from two to three active battalions. During the following year, however, the Austrians invaded Illyria and the great majority of the former Grenzers abandoned the French to re-enter the ranks of the Austrian Army.

Until 22 May 1810, the Illyrian Chasseurs continued to wear their old Austrian uniforms; on that date, however, a new French-style dress was introduced. This comprised a standard black shako and a medium blue single-breasted coat; its collar, pointed cuffs, frontal piping and turn-backs were in regimental colours. The uniform was completed with a white waistcoat, medium blue trousers and black half-boots. Regimental colours were as follows: red for 1st Regiment, crimson for 2nd Regiment, yellow for 3rd Regiment, violet for 4th Regiment, sky blue for 5th Regiment and green for 6th Regiment.

In order to have some battalions of Illyrian Chasseurs available for military

Infantrymen of the Northern Legion; from left to right: grenadier, fusilier and voltigeur.

service outside their home territories, in 1811, Napoleon ordered the formation of **Croatian Provisional Regiments**, created by assembling the active battalions provided for overseas or non-domestic service by each regiment of Illyrian Chasseurs. Since each regiment provided one or two battalions for external service, it was possible to create four Croatian Provisional Regiments with two battalions each. The battalions had the same internal structure as the French light infantry battalions with one company of carabiniers, one company of voltigeurs and four companies of chasseurs.

The first three Croatian Provisional Regiments fought with great determination as part of the French Army in the campaigns of 1812 and 1813; the fourth, was mostly deployed in Italy and saw no combat. All four regiments were disbanded in January 1814, mostly due to the heavy losses suffered.

In January 1812, to be easily distinguishable from their parent units of the Illyrian Chasseurs, the Croatian Provisional Regiments received

Trooper of the 1st Lancer Regiment of the Vistula Legion (later 7th Regiment of Lancers).

a distinctive green uniform: this was like that worn by the French light infantry regiments, but entirely in medium green (instead of medium blue) and with yellow facings/piping. The trousers had a yellow side-stripe and yellow decorative knots on the front.

In the early months of 1810, Napoleon decided to raise another regular military unit from his Illyrian Provinces. This was made up of soldiers from the non-frontier areas of Illyria. The new corps was known as **Illyrian Regiment** and was structured with five battalions of light infantry (four active and one in depot). The unit served with distinction in Russia, where it suffered severe losses; it was disbanded on 17 November 1813.

The Illyrian Regiment was dressed exactly like the French light infantry, but with red collar and pointed cuffs piped in white; in addition, its members had red shoulder wings piped in white on their coats.

IRREGULAR SOLDIERS

Illyrians

In addition to the regular units described above, the French also recruited sizeable numbers of irregulars from the Illyrian Provinces. These could belong to the Serezaners or to the Pandours. The Serezaners were first raised in the 1790s, by the Austrian authorities, from Bosnian refugees who had settled on Croatian lands. They were each organised into companies of 200 men, which were attached to the regiments of grenzers. Each regiment of frontier infantry had its own company of Serezaners, which acted as scouts in war time and as frontier guards in peace time.

The irregular soldiers did not have uniforms but wore their national dress that comprised red pointed hat during winter, or red cap during summer, white or blue loose shirt, red or blue waistcoat decorated with silver rings and buttons, loose-fitting trousers and soft leather shoes.

Above left: Soldier of the 1st Regiment of Illyrian Chasseurs.

Above middle: Soldier of the Croatian Provisional Regiments.

Above right: Trooper of the Croatian Hussars.

Like the Pandours, and the semi-regular units recruited in the Ionian Islands, the Serezaners were armed with a bewildering variety of locally manufactured traditional weapons: long-barrelled muskets, pistols, curved sabres and knives.

Corps of Dalmatian Pandours

The Pandours made up an irregular corps of militarised policemen who were tasked (since 1748) with guarding the Balkan frontier of the Austrian Empire, in Bosnia, from the incursions of the Ottomans. On 17 March 1810, they were reorganised by the French as part of the military forces of the Illyrian Provinces and received the new designation of Corps of Dalmatian Pandours. In exchange for their services, these irregulars were exempted from the usual labour obligations of Balkan peasants; they trained every Sunday after Mass and were excellent marksmen.

The Corps of Dalmatian Pandours consisted of nine companies.

- Each corps included one colonel, three battalion commanders, five adjutant-majors, nine captains, one paymaster, nine lieutenants, nine sub-lieutenants, 27 sergeant-majors and 54 sergeants.
- A single company comprised one captain, one lieutenant, one sub-lieutenant, three sergeant-majors, six sergeants and 36 or 48 rankers (including two drummers).

When the Austrians invaded the Illyrian Provinces in 1813, the Pandours were the only Balkan soldiers to remain loyal to the French; their corps was disbanded soon after the victory of the Austrians.

On the day of their reorganisation, in March 1810, the Pandours received the following uniform: red turban, red waistcoat, red dolman jacket with silver lacing and lambswool trimming, blue trousers and brown sandals. This was later replaced by a new uniform including standard black shako, dark blue dolman jacket with red collar and round cuffs having white frontal frogging, dark blue trousers with white side-stripe and decorative knots on the front, brown sandals.

Corps of Albanian Pandours

In addition to the Dalmatian Pandours, in June 1810, the French authorities also organised an independent Corps of Albanian Pandours that was tasked with protecting the southern Bay of Cattaro from the incursions of Montenegrin raiders. This unit consisted of six companies (later increased to eight) that were all disbanded by 1813. The Albanian Pandours wore the same uniform, introduced in 1810, as the Dalmatian Pandours.

Croatian Hussars

On 23 February 1813, a regiment of hussars was raised by the French from the border regions of Croatia. It consisted of six squadrons with two troops each and was equipped at the expense of the citizens living in the Illyrian Provinces. The unit took part in some minor military actions before being disbanded in November 1813. The surviving elements of the regiment were reorganised as five companies of Croatian Pioneers, which were dissolved in April 1814.

Black Pioneers

On 11 May 1803, Napoleon created a Battalion of Black Pioneers inside his army by assembling several coloured POWs from the Caribbean island of Haiti (former supporters of the revolutionary leader Toussaint L'ouverture) and a short-lived battalion of African Chasseurs that had been formed for the Indian campaign of 1803. The battalion served with distinction in Italy; as a result, in August 1806, it was transferred to the Neapolitan Army of which it became part (at that time the Kingdom of Naples was a puppet state of France, ruled by Napoleon's brother Joseph). In November 1806, the corps was transformed into a regiment of line infantry known as Real Africano or Royal African.

Chapter 5

The Cuirassiers

HISTORY AND ORGANISATION

According to the reorganisation of 1793, the French cavalry comprised a total of 25 heavy regiments that were commonly known as *cavalerie de ligne* or line cavalry. The troopers of these units did not have helmets or cuirasses, but were easily distinguishable from the rest of the French cavalrymen since they were armed with straight swords and wore tall leather boots. Traditionally, the heavy cavalry regiments were led by officers from some of the most important members of the French aristocracy and thus the political events of the Revolution, which saw these leaders swept away, had a great impact on the command structure of these units. The proud regimental titles – which were based on well-established traditions – were abolished and the revolutionary government did its best to eradicate the aristocratic character from the French heavy cavalry.

During the Revolutionary Wars, the French line cavalry did not perform particularly well, and its lack of cohesion and training became apparent on several occasions. After becoming First Consul, Napoleon reformed the heavy cavalry to be much more effective on the battlefield. He considered transforming his line cavalrymen into cuirassiers in order to distinguish them tactically from the medium cavalry of the dragoons. Like Frederick the Great, the First Consul was strongly convinced that having a certain number of mounted regiments equipped with metal cuirasses could represent a great advantage when fighting large cavalry battles. In addition, he considered cuirassiers as a shock force that could break the infantry formations of the enemy with well-planned and well-conducted frontal charges.

For these reasons, in October 1801, the First Consul transformed the 1st Line Cavalry Regiment into the 1st Regiment of Cuirassiers by assigning helmets and breastplates to its members. After a short experiment with this single unit, Napoleon restructured his heavy cavalry in September 1802. Until that time, each regiment of line cavalry had consisted of three squadrons. He ordered the reduction of regiments from 25 to 18 but increased the number of squadrons in each unit from three to four. Of the 18 new heavy regiments, six were to be equipped with cuirasses. By the end of 1803, however, only 12 of the new units had been given cuirasses and the remaining ones were deprived of their heavy cavalry status. From 1803, the core of the French heavy cavalry started to consist of 12 cuirassier regiments equipped with full cuirasses (including breastplate and backplate) and helmets.

- The staff of each regiment consisted of one colonel, one major, two lieutenant-colonels, one quartermaster, one surgeon-major, one chaplain, two adjutants, one trumpet-major and five master-artisans.
- The four squadrons that made up a regiment were structured on two companies each. A single company comprised one captain, one lieutenant, one second-lieutenant, one senior staff-sergeant, four junior staff-sergeants, one fourrier, eight brigadiers, one trumpeter and 82 troopers. A single company consisted of two troops and thus had a very flexible structure.
- In 1807, the composition of the regimental staff was one colonel, one major, two squadron commanders, two adjutant-majors, one paymaster-quartermaster, one surgeon-major, one assistant-major, two sub-assistant majors, two adjutants, one trumpet-major, one veterinary surgeon and six artisans (the latter being cobblers, tailors, armourers and saddlers).

Above left: NCO of the cuirassiers wearing bicorn. (Photo: 2ème Régiment de Dragons, © Pauline Wilmotte)

Above right: Trooper (centre) and trumpeters (right and left) of the cuirassiers. The central figure has the new M1812 dress, while the musicians have pre-1812 uniforms in regimental colour.

In March 1807, the number of squadrons in each cuirassier regiment was increased from four to five. Maintaining in service a unit of heavy cavalry equipped with helmets and cuirasses was extremely costly and thus, during the period taken into account, the number of cuirassier regiments was not greatly expanded.

In December 1807, by assembling several detachments from existing regiments deployed in southern France for the upcoming invasion of Spain, a new *Régiment Provisorie de Grosse Cavalerie* or Provisional Regiment of Heavy Cavalry was formed. In 1808, the new regiment, after it absorbed another new Provisional Regiment of Heavy Cavalry, became the new 13th Regiment of Cuirassiers. A third Régiment Provisorie de Grosse Cavalerie came into existence during 1808 but this, unlike the previous two, never became part of a permanent unit.

Dutch Army

In 1810, the Kingdom of Holland, ruled by Napoleon's brother Louis, ceased to be an independent state and was absorbed into the French Empire. As a result, the best units of the disbanded Dutch Army became

Above left: Cuirassier with helmet and cuirass. (Photo: 2ème Régiment de Dragons, © Pauline Wilmotte)

Above middle: NCO of the cuirassiers wearing helmet. (Photo: 2ème Régiment de Dragons, © Pauline Wilmotte)

Above right: Cuirassier with helmet and cuirass. (Photo: 2ème Régiment de Dragons, © Pauline Wilmotte)

part of the French Army. Among these was the 2nd Regiment of Cuirassiers, which was transformed into the 14th Regiment of Cuirassiers.

Performance

During the Napoleonic Wars, the cuirassier units fought with great distinction on several occasions, participating in all the most important pitched battles. They distinguished themselves at the Battle of Eylau (7 and 8 February 1807) when – under command of Murat, Napoleon's greatest cavalry commander – one of their impressive frontal charges saved the Emperor from a bitter defeat.

During the Russian campaign of 1812, the French heavy cavalrymen conducted another impressive charge at the Battle of Borodino (7 September), one of the bloodiest clashes in the history of the Napoleonic Wars.

With the first restoration of the Bourbons that followed Napoleon's first abdication, the number of cuirassier regiments was reduced to 12. During the Belgian Campaign of 1815, the French heavy cavalry fought with desperate courage at Quatre Bras, and at Waterloo it tried to break the defensive squares of Wellington's infantry. The cuirassiers, commanded by Napoleon's Marshal Ney, charged several times against the 'thin red line' but were always repulsed and suffered heavy casualties. Wellington was greatly impressed by their courage, and officers admired their perfect discipline and great horsemanship. After the second restoration of the Bourbons, the cuirassiers continued to be an important component of the French Army's cavalry.

UNIFORMS AND EQUIPMENT

The helmet of the cuirassiers consisted of an iron cap surrounded by a black fur turban and surmounted by a copper crest. On the front, it had a black visor with the external edge in copper while on the left side, it had a copper fitting sustaining a red plume. On the frontal point of the crest, there was a black pompom surmounted by a tuft of the same colour. Over the crest there was a black horsehair mane and the helmet had a copper chinscale that departed on each side from a copper disk decorated with a five-pointed star.

The helmets of the officers had the pompom placed on the frontal point of the crest in copper and not in black wool.

The helmets of the trumpeters had the tuft and the horsehair mane in white.

The helmets of the French cuirassiers, being in clear Neoclassical-style, were extremely elegant but quite uncomfortable to wear.

The cuirass, made up of a breastplate and a backplate, was the most distinctive element of the French heavy cavalry's equipment; it was made of iron and was produced in three different models during the Napoleonic Period. The first model, designed in 1802, had a blunt angle at its base. It had 34 copper rivets driven into the perimeters of both the breastplate and the backplate. The cuirass was put on by first hooking the ends of its brass-scaled shoulder straps to some apposite spherical copper buttons that were

NCO of the cuirassiers. (Photo: 2ème Régiment de Dragons, © Pauline Wilmotte)

Trumpeter of the cuirassiers with pre-1812 dress in regimental colour (yellow for this unit, which is the 7th Regiment of Cuirassiers).

riveted to the front of the breastplate. The two halves of the cuirass were then fastened together at the waist by means of a copper-buckled, white leather belt that was secured to the back plate by twin copper rivets at each end.

In 1806, a new model of cuirass was introduced; this differed from the previous one in that the bottom of the breastplate was now rounded. In 1809, the third model of cuirass came into use; this had a more rounded profile and was slightly shorter when compared with the previous one. The officers' cuirasses were decorated with a deeply engraved single line of laurel branches placed 3cm from the external edge. The engraved line was gilded like the scaled shoulder straps.

The trumpeters did not wear cuirasses.

Inside all the cuirasses there was a padded protective garment known as a *fraise*, which was red with white external edging. In 1803, soon after their formation, the French cuirassiers were given a tunic that was similar to the one that the line cavalry wore. Known as the *habit-surtout*, it was dark blue and single-breasted. The tunic had collar, round cuffs, cuff flaps and turn-backs in regimental colour. The collar and the cuff flaps were piped in dark blue, while the front of the *habit-surtout* and the vertical 'false' pockets placed on the back of the tails were piped in regimental colour. On the turn-backs, there were decorative dark blue flaming grenades. The shoulder straps of the tunic were dark blue with piping in regimental colour. The buttons of the *habit-surtout* were all made of pewter and were stamped with the distinctive number of each regiment.

In 1809, a new model of tunic came into use; this had mid-thigh-length tails without pockets and turn-backs. The new *habit-surtout* was never particularly appreciated by the soldiers and was replaced in 1812 by one that was very short-skirted and had both turn-backs and vertical simulated pockets.

The tunic introduced in 1812 marked the last change in the development of a suitable *habit-surtout* that could be easily worn by cavalrymen using a cuirass. The officers' dress had the buttons and the flaming grenade patches in silver. As an alternative to the *habit-surtout*, for service dress, the cuirassiers could wear a simpler surtout without piping on the front. In 1812, a new model came into use; this had red piping to the collar, cuffs and on the front, in addition to turn-backs of the same colour. The surtout was usually worn with a black bicorn or with the fatigue cap known as the bonnet de police, which was dark blue with white piping and frontal tassel, bearing on the front a flaming grenade embroidered in white. The habit-surtout always had red-fringed epaulettes, which were silver and showed rank for officers. The NCOs' rank was shown by simple stripes of white cloth that were applied on the lower sleeves, while the years of service of both NCOs and rankers were shown by red inverted chevrons that were applied on the left upper sleeve.

The trumpeters, who had no cuirass, wore a habit-surtout that was in regimental colour and that had additional stripes of white lace on the front as well as on the collar and cuffs. Their epaulettes were white. The dress regulations of 1812 attempted to regularise musicians' uniforms by introducing a standard Imperial livery to be worn by all of them. This consisted of a dark green single-breasted jacket ornamented with stripes of lace having alternate yellow and green segments. The yellow segments were decorated with an interwoven dark green crowned 'N', while the dark green ones were decorated with an interwoven yellow Imperial Eagle.

On parade, all the cuirassiers wore deer-hide breeches. On campaign these were replaced with practical overalls that were made of linen and could be of different colours (varying from light grey to grey-brown). These were closed by cloth-covered buttons placed down the length of the outer seams.

The parade breeches of the officers were of chamois hide and were usually replaced, on service, with dark blue linen breeches. The outfit of the cuirassiers was completed by their tall grenadier boots made of black leather and by their white gloves. The belt equipment of all ranks was white leather. The saddlecoth was of two parts consisting of a white half-shabraque made of sheepskin that was edged with small triangles of cloth in regimental colour worn over a dark blue shabraque edged in white that had a white flaming grenade on the back corner. Since their creation, the cuirassiers had been armed with heavy cavalry swords each with a straight blade; these were of the Year IX model (1800) during 1803–05 and of the Year XI (1802) model during 1806–15. Until 1812, the French cuirassiers were equipped with a couple of flintlock pistols; these could be of the Year IX or of the Year XIII (1804) model. From 1812, they started to be equipped with a flintlock musketoon of the Year XI model, which had its own bayonet. The ammunition for this weapon was carried on the back, in a black leather pouch, suspended from a white leather crossbelt. The musketoon was not given to officers and trumpeters, who were armed with sword and pistols.

Chapter 6

The Carabiniers

HISTORY AND ORGANISATION

The second half of the 17th century saw the development of a new cavalry troop type, that of the carabiniers. The carabiniers' name was derived from their main weapon, a *carabine* or carbine. In the early decades of its existence, this was a shortened version of the infantry's flintlock muskets that could be employed by cavalrymen firing from horseback. The French understood the potential of this new cavalry weapon, which could significantly augment the firepower of mounted troops. Until that point, the cavalry corps of the European armies had mostly been equipped with light firearms (flintlock pistols) with quite a short range.

The last decades of the 17th century brought a series of experiments that tested the tactical role of the new carabiniers. Over time, it became clear that elite cavalry soldiers armed with carbines could be extremely useful on the battlefield, since they could support the other horsemen armed with swords with an accurate fire comparable to that of the infantry. Initially, only two carabiniers were added to each company of light cavalry, but in 1691, each light cavalry regiment was ordered to have an entire company of carabiniers to act as vanguard. In November 1693, following the French victory at the Battle of Neerwinden that was mostly decided by the carabiniers, Louis XIV decided to create an autonomous unit of carabiniers inside his army: the *Carabiniers du Roi* or King's Carabiniers.

King's Carabiniers

This unit was formed by assembling all the carabinier companies that already existed in the French Army. It was a very large establishment, consisting of 100 companies of 30 men each. The companies were structured into 20 squadrons, each with five companies, and thus was comparable to a standard cavalry regiment. The members of the *Carabiniers du Roi* were selected from the best elements of the French mounted units: they had to be at least 1.73cm tall, unmarried and of good character. They were paid higher wages than the ordinary cavalry and soon attained elite status inside the French military forces. One of the finest cavalry corps of the French Army was born. During the 18th century, the carabiniers changed denomination several times, but were always commanded by an important member of the royal family (usually the king's younger brother).

In 1776, to cut costs, the five brigades of carabiniers were reduced to a single regiment with eight squadrons; each with five officers and 145 troopers each. The corps remained a very 'aristocratic' unit and continued to enjoy an elite status. In 1779, the carabiniers were reorganised again, this time into two brigades with five squadrons each; a single squadron now consisted of six officers and 156 troopers. In 1788, shortly before the outbreak of the Revolution, the two brigades were transformed into regiments having four squadrons each.

The two regiments of carabiniers were always brigaded together and were practically inseparable; they made up an elite force of 'shock' heavy cavalry, which was to be used only during the most important pitched battles. After the outbreak of the Revolution and the removal of the king from effective power, the new republican authorities considered disbanding the two regiments of carabiniers, since they represented the power of the king and aristocracy inside the French Army. After further discussion, however, it became clear that it would have been pointless to disband some of the best mounted units at

Carabinier with pre-1810 parade dress.

the country's disposal and thus the two corps continued to exist. They received the new denomination of Grenadiers of the Mounted Troops and were reorganised as regiments with two squadrons of two companies each.

The years of the Revolutionary Wars were characterised by a series of incidents for the carabiniers, since they remained strong supporters of the king and not of the new republican authorities. The two regiments were on the verge of being disbanded on several occasions, especially when all the aristocrats were expelled from the French Army following the execution of the king. Ultimately, the carabiniers were able to survive this difficult period and to distinguish themselves during several pitched battles.

After becoming First Consul in 1799, Napoleon paid special attention to the regiments of carabiniers. He appointed some of his relatives, or his most loyal supporters, as officers in the two units and distributed weapons of honour to many carabiniers to secure their loyalty. After the proclamation of the Empire, the carabiniers hoped to become part of the newly created Imperial Guard due to their support for the new political regime as well as to their traditional elite status. However, the Imperial Guard already included a regiment of heavy cavalry with the same features as the carabiniers (the Regiment of Mounted Grenadiers).

Despite never becoming part of the Imperial Guard, the regiments of carabiniers continued to enjoy a higher military status than the cuirassier regiments of the French heavy cavalry. Organisationally, the carabiniers were subject to the same changes that were progressively introduced for the cuirassiers. In August 1806, their two regiments were ordered to have four squadrons each, a single squadron being formed by two companies; in March 1807, the number of squadrons was increased to five.

That year, the carabiniers fought with distinction at the Battle of Friedland, during which they charged with great determination. Since the Revolutionary Wars, they were known as the 'Army's butchers' because of the violence of their attacks. During 1809, the carabiniers participated in the campaign that was fought against the Austrians and took part in the bloody Battle of Wagram, during which they suffered severe losses. Napoleon, knowing it was extremely difficult to replace fallen carabiniers with men of the same quality, upgraded the equipment after the events of Wagram.

The massive bearskin that had been worn was replaced with a helmet, the dark blue uniforms were substituted with new white ones and cuirasses were distributed to all members of the two regiments (which now lost their mounted grenadier character and practically became cuirassier corps). After receiving a new uniform and a new equipment (their muskets were replaced with musketoons), the carabinier regiments were reviewed and a new internal structure with just four squadrons was imposed. By 1811, the carabiniers had completed their transformation and were ready to participate in the Russian Campaign. There they fought with enormous courage at the Battle of Borodino before suffering severe losses during the long retreat that marked Napoleon's defeat. By the end of the campaign almost all members of the two regiments had died.

In the early months of 1813, the Emperor had to rebuild his army practically from zero, by using all the resources at his disposal. The two regiments of carabiniers were reconstituted with an establishment of five squadrons each, but their quality was no longer comparable to the pre-1812 regiments since new members were inexperienced recruits.

During the German campaign of 1813, the carabiniers suffered significant losses and required re-organisation again for the French campaign of 1814. During that event, they took part in several engagements until Napoleon was forced to abdicate. With the first restoration of the Bourbons,

Carabinier with pre-1810 campaign dress.

Carabinier with M1810 uniform.

the aristocratic status of the carabiniers was reintroduced and the regiments were restructured with four squadrons in each. When the Emperor returned from his exile in 1815, the carabiniers were more than happy to join his cause and to renounce their new royal status. The long years of the Napoleonic campaigns had changed their nature. Like the cuirassiers, the carabiniers charged with great determination during the Battle of Waterloo in the hope of breaking the squares of Wellington's line infantry. In the end, however, their efforts were meagre when compared with that of the whole French cavalry taking part.

With the second restoration of the Bourbons, the number of carabinier regiments in the French Army was reduced from two to one. The elite heavy cavalrymen remained part of the French Army until 1871, after having achieved their objective of becoming part of the Imperial Guard during the years of Napoleon III's 'Second Empire'.

UNIFORMS AND EQUIPMENT

The pre-1810 uniform of the carabiniers was very similar to that of the Imperial Guard's Mounted Grenadiers. Its most distinctive element was a tall black bearskin of 31.8cm height with having white wool cords plaited into flounders and tasselled at each end. The top of the headgear, at the back, was covered with a round piece of red felt cloth decorated with a white cross. On the left side of the bearskin, departing from a tricolour cockade, there was a red plume (half red and half white for trumpeters). With full dress, the carabiniers wore a dark blue *habit* coat, which had a dark blue standing collar piped in red and red round cuffs piped in dark blue. The frontal lapels of the coat were red, while the cuff flaps were red with dark blue piping for the 1st Regiment and dark blue with red piping for the 2nd Regiment. The turn-backs of the tails were red and there were horizontal false pockets on the back coat, which were decorated with three buttons and with red piping. All the buttons of the *habit* were of white metal and showed a flaming grenade badge. The dark blue badge was repeated on the turn-backs.

In 1808, the colour of the flaming grenades embroidered on the turn-backs was changed to white. On the shoulders of the tunic, there were red-fringed epaulettes, a distinctive element of the grenadier dress – these became white in 1808. For most types of duties, the full dress habit was replaced with a dark blue single-breasted *surtout*, which was cut away high on the stomach. This had dark blue collar and cuffs piped in red. The front was piped in red and its turn-backs were red with dark blue decorative flaming grenades. Underneath both the habit and the surtout, a white-sleeved waistcoat was worn. Two types of breeches were issued to each carabinier: the first were made of off-white sheep's leather and the second were made of canvas. The former were used on parade while the latter – being dark blue – were fastened from top to bottom up the sides with bone buttons (these being in common use on campaign).

Trumpeters were dressed like the other carabiniers, but their uniform was in reversed colours: red with dark blue facings. In addition, the coat had white piping on collar, cuffs and front lapels. The epaulettes were white. The outfit of the carabiniers was complete with tall black leather boots and white leather gloves with gauntlets. The epaulettes of officers were silver and showed their rank. The NCO rank was shown by simple stripes of white cloth that were applied on the lower sleeves, while the years of service of both NCOs and rankers were shown by red inverted chevrons that were applied on the left upper sleeve. The belt equipment of all ranks was white leather. The saddlecoth consisted of a white half-shabraque made of sheepskin that was edged with small triangles of cloth in red and of a dark blue shabraque edged in white that had a white flaming grenade on the back corner. The carabiniers also had the fatigue cap known as the bonnet de police: this was dark blue with white piping and frontal tassel. On the front, the cap bore a flaming grenade embroidered in white.

The new cuirassier-style uniform, introduced in 1810, was extremely elegant and quite unusual for the Napoleonic cavalry, since it was white. The helmet was made of yellow brass and decorated with a frontal band in white metal, which ended at the bosses for the chinscale. These bosses were of a rayed sunburst design with a central brass five-pointed star. The frontal brass band of the helmet was decorated with a brass crowned 'N' and was swept up into a point placed below the front of the crest. A narrow white metal band continued from behind the chinscale bosses around the rear base of the skull. The rear neck guard of the helmet had an edging made of white metal. The crest was decorated with fluting and was surmounted by a large red caterpillar of padded horsehair. The chinscale consisted of 16 rows of white metal. The steel cuirass was heavy and costly. It had a yellow brass plate soldered to its external surfaces with a 2.5cm bare steel border all around, which was embellished with brass rivets. The breastplate and the backplate were held together by a belt of natural leather held in place by a brass buckle as well as two shoulder straps that were covered with brass scales (these terminated in brass plates pierced with two fixing holes for studs). The inside of the cuirass was padded with a *fraise* of light blue cloth with white external edging. The *fraise* protruded above, below and in the armholes of the cuirass.

The helmets and cuirasses of the officers were made of a redder and more copper-rich alloy than those of the troopers; in addition, they had silvered fixtures and fittings. The officers' breastplates bore a silver sunburst decoration on the front, with a five-pointed star at its centre. Under the cuirass, a short-tailed and single-breasted white jacket was worn, which had standing collar and round cuffs in light blue with white piping. The front edge of the jacket was piped in light blue. Its short tails had light blue turn-backs decorated with white flaming grenade badges. On the back of the tails were vertical false pockets finished with light blue piping and three buttons. The epaulettes worn on the shoulders were red with a white braid edging all around the top of their strap.

The two regiments were distinguishable only by the colour of their cuff flaps; these were white with light blue piping for the 1st Regiment and light blue with white piping for the 2nd Regiment. The breeches remained the campaign issue and were brown or grey.

The trumpeters did not have the cuirass and instead wore a jacket with reversed colours (light blue with white facings) and with white piping on collar and cuffs. Their epaulettes were white, like the massive crest of their helmets. The epaulettes of officers were silver and showed their rank. The NCOs' rank was shown by simple stripes of white cloth that were applied on the lower sleeves, while the years of service of

Above left: **Carabinier with M1810 dress.**

Above right: **Trumpeter of the carabiniers with M1812 uniform (Imperial Livery).**

NCOs and rankers were shown by red inverted chevrons that were applied on the left upper sleeve. The black leather boots, white leather gloves and white leather belt equipment remained unchanged.

The saddlecoth consisted of a white half-shabraque made of sheepskin that was edged with small triangles of cloth in light blue and of a light blue shabraque edged in white that had a white flaming grenade on the back corner.

The new dress regulations of 1812 attempted to regularise the uniforms of the musicians, by introducing a standard Imperial Livery to be worn by all. It consisted of a dark green single-breasted jacket ornamented with stripes of lace having alternate yellow and green segments. The yellow segments were decorated with an interwoven dark green crowned 'N', while the dark green ones were decorated with an interwoven yellow Imperial Eagle. Until 1810, the carabiniers were armed with heavy cavalry swords of the 'Year IV' (1795) and 'Year XI' (1802) model, which had a flaming grenade device stamped on their guard. In addition, they also carried a couple of 'Year IX' (1800) or 'Year VIII' (1799) flintlock pistols and a 'dragoon' flintlock musket of the 'Year IX' or 'Year VIII' model. In 1810, the carabiniers replaced their straight swords with slightly curved sabres and their muskets with a cavalry musketoon of the 'Year IX' model.

Chapter 7

The Dragoons

HISTORY AND ORGANISATION

In 1786, there were 24 regiments of dragoons in the French Army. Two years later, the regiments were reduced to 18, when the royal government decided to create the new corps of mounted chasseurs. Six of the existing dragoon units were converted to mounted chasseurs. In 1793, the new republican government increased the number of dragoon regiments to 21. Napoleon, who appreciated the tactical flexibility of the dragoons and who liked to employ them as infantrymen, augmented the number of dragoon units soon after becoming First Consul. In 1803, nine new regiments of dragoons were created, bringing the total number to 30. This figure remained stable until 1811, when six dragoon regiments were converted into lancer units (*see* the next chapter for more details). Of the nine new regiments of dragoons that were formed by Napoleon in 1803, six were former units of line cavalry and three were former units of hussars.

According to the organisation prescribed in September 1803, each regiment of dragoons was to be structured on four squadrons and each squadron was to consist of two companies. The staff of each regiment comprised one colonel, one major, two squadron commanders, one adjutant sub-officer, one staff sergeant, one brigadier-trumpeter, one brigadier-drummer, one brigadier-sapper and eight sappers. This small squad of sappers was tasked with 'clearing the way' for its unit during marches and with building field fortifications. The mixed infantry/cavalry nature of the dragoon regiments was characterised by the presence of sappers inside each regimental staff and also in the internal structure of each single company.

According to the organisation introduced in 1803, a company of dragoons consisted of one captain, one lieutenant, two sub-lieutenants, one brigadier-fourrier, four brigadiers (corporals), one trumpeter, one drummer, 54 mounted rankers and 36 dismounted rankers. Each company of dragoons was a mixed unit of foot and horse infantry with a trumpeter for the mounted rankers and a drummer for the foot rankers. The composition of the regimental staff changed very little during 1803–11, with only the abolition of the staff sergeant role in 1808.

In 1811, the following elements were added to each regimental staff: one quartermaster, two adjutant-majors and one major-surgeon. In 1807, after having fought with great distinction during several campaigns, all the French dragoons were given horses and thus the specific 'mixed' nature of infantry/cavalry was lost.

During 1803–06, Napoleon experimented tactically with the dragoons. In case of war mobilisation, foot soldiers of the various regiments were detached from their parent units and were assembled into temporary foot brigades. At the camp of Boulogne, built for the planned invasion of Great Britain in 1803, the foot dragoons were assembled into five foot brigades (provided by three or four regiments). For the campaign of 1805 that culminated with the Battle of Austerlitz, the foot dragoons were assembled into four temporary regiments with two battalions each. Another independent battalion of foot dragoons was organised, in 1805, inside the French military forces fighting against the Austrians in northern Italy. Finally, for the Prussian campaign of 1806, two temporary regiments of foot dragoons with two battalions each were created.

Napoleon was not particularly enthusiastic about his dismounted dragoons' combat performances and thus – after having captured enough horses from his enemies – decided to terminate all the experiments

Above left: Officer of the dragoons wearing pre-1812 dress. (Photo Le Livre, l'Histoire et l'Obusier, © Rose-Hélène Ledanseur)

Above middle: Officer of the dragoons with pre-1812 dress.

Above right: Officer of the dragoons serving as 'Aide-de-camp'. (Photo: 2ème Régiment de Dragons, © Pauline Wilmotte)

and to give horses to all his dragoons. From 1807, the dragoons distinguished themselves in all the major battles such as Eylau (7 and 8 February 1807) and Friedland on 14 June 1807 (both fought against the Russians), or Wagram (5 and 6 July 1809, fought against the Austrians). The dragoons made a great contribution to Napoleon's war efforts in Spain, where they countered local insurgents effectively thanks to their mixed cavalry/infantry training.

The Russian campaign of 1812 and the German campaign of 1813 had a terrible impact on the dragoon regiments, many of which were completely destroyed. The Emperor re-built the dragoon units after these events, but with young recruits who had very little combat experience. Following the first restoration of the Bourbons, the number of dragoon regiments in the French Army was reduced to 15. Most participated in the Belgian Campaign of 1815 that culminated with Napoleon's defeat at Waterloo.

UNIFORMS AND EQUIPMENT

The distinctive headgear of the dragoons was an elegant helmet in Neoclassical style, known as *Casque à la Minerve*, or Minerva Helmet, since it resembled the headgear worn by the mythical ancient goddess. It was made of a yellow alloy very similar to copper and was encircled by a brown fur turban. On the helmet's top, there was a heavily embossed copper crest supporting a black horsehair mane, while on the front of the headgear was a black leather peak that could have a copper external edge. The chinstrap could be of black leather or covered with copper scales. It attached to each side of the headgear from a copper disk decorated with a five-pointed star. The turban could be pointed on the front and could have two stripes of copper on the external edges. On the frontal point of the crest, on top of a copper pompom, there was a small tuft made of black wool. On parade, a plume was inserted in an apposite copper holder placed just forward of the left-hand chinstrap disk. The plume was white for most of the regiments, but its colour varied from unit to unit (red and green being quite popular).

The 1812 dress regulations attempted to regularise the use of plumes, and prescribed that plumes had to be replaced with simple discs of cloth. The cloth was a specific colour for each squadron: red for the 1st, sky-blue for the 2nd, orange for the 3rd and violet for the 4th. This scheme of colours had to be adopted by each regiment for all its squadrons. The gradual substitution of the plumes with discs happened slowly and in 1814, it was not uncommon to see dragoon helmets with coloured plumes.

According to a decree promulgated by Napoleon on 10 October 1801, the 1st Company of the 1st Squadron of each dragoon regiment was to be known as the Elite Company, since its members were the most experienced veterans of their unit. These soldiers had the privilege of wearing distinctive headgear. Their massive black bearskin, at 31.8cm tall, had red wool cords plaited into flounders and tasselled at each end. The top of the headgear, at the back, was covered with a round piece of red felt cloth decorated with a white cross. On the left side of the bearskin, departing from a tricolour cockade, was a red plume. The soldiers of the Elite Company, in grenadier tradition, also had red-fringed epaulettes that distinguished them from the standard dragoons.

The few sappers that were attached to each regiment of dragoons wore uniforms with the same specific distinctions as the Elite Company. They used the bearskin as headgear and their coats featured red epaulettes. In addition, they had a specific badge consisting of two crossed axes embroidered in red on the upper sleeves. Their uniform featured a white leather apron. Their specific equipment included a massive axe and the white leather crossbelt sustaining their ammunition pouch had a distinctive brass badge on the front (consisting of a flaming grenade above two crossed axes). Sometimes the bearskin of the Elite Company and sappers featured a brass flaming grenade on the front, or could be replaced with a smaller 'light cavalry' busby having its same main features.

The trumpeters used the same headgear as the ordinary dragoons, but with white horsehair mane and white tuft. On parade they wore plumes that were white on the

Ensign of the dragoons. (Photo: 2ème Régiment de Dragons, © Pauline Wilmotte)

Above left: Dragoons of the 17th Regiment with M1812 uniform.

Above right: Sapper of the dragoons with pre-1812 dress. (Photo: Le Livre, l'Histoire et l'Obusier, © Rose-Hélène Ledanseur)

bottom half and in regimental colour on the upper half. The trumpeter of the Elite Company could have a white bearskin instead of the usual black one. On service or campaign the helmet and the bearskin were usually replaced by the bonnet de police fatigue cap. This, as for all the units of the French Army, was composed of a turban and a 'flame' that were dark green for the dragoons. The uppermost edge of the turban was piped in white, while the flame was piped in regimental colour and ended in a white tassel. The front of the cap bore a flaming grenade badge embroidered in white or regimental colour.

The dress regulations of 1812 introduced a new model of fatigue cap known as the *pokalem*. It was the same colour as, and had the basic features of, the bonnet de police, but consisted of a large round turban with a flat top and ear flaps. The pokalem, according to the official dress regulations, was to replace the bonnet de police as the fatigue cap of both the heavy and the medium cavalry. In practice, it was used sporadically, since the bonnet de police continued to be worn after 1812. With full dress, the dragoons wore a dark green habit coat, which had a standing collar and round cuffs in regimental colour. Its front lapels were in regimental colour, while the cuff flaps were dark green with piping in regimental colour. The turn-backs of the tails were in regimental colour, while the tails had vertical or horizontal false pockets decorated with three buttons and piped in regimental colour. All the buttons of the habit were made of pewter and were embossed with the distinctive number of each regiment. The coat had dark green shoulder straps piped in regimental colour. On the coat tail turn-backs, there were decorative flaming grenade badges embroidered in dark green. The areas of the coat in regimental colour, their position and the direction of the false pockets on the tails (vertical or horizontal) distinguished the various regiments. The facings were piped in dark green other than when the regimental colour was dark green, and in this instance they were piped in a 'secondary' regimental colour.

During 1799–1812, the general cut of the dragoons' habit changed very slightly, becoming slimmer and shorter; its turn-backs, for example, became false and stitched along their entire length. The illusion of true turn-backs was initially maintained by the retention of the triangle of dark green cloth visible beneath their juncture, but by 1810 this practice had ceased. Under the habit, a simple white waistcoat was worn, which had twin pockets at the waist and a single row of buttons on the front.

For most duties the full dress habit was replaced with a dark green single-breasted *surtout*, which was cut away high on the stomach. This had dark green collar and cuffs piped in regimental colour. The piping on its front and its turn-backs were in regimental colour with dark green decorative flaming grenades.

The new dress regulations promulgated on 8 February 1812 prescribed the abolition of the old-fashioned habit and the introduction of the new habit-veste. This new item of clothing differed from the

Above left: Sapper of the 7th Regiment of Dragoons with pre-1812 uniform and busby.

Above right: Drummer of the dragoons, wearing the distinctive uniform with reversed colours.
(Photo: Le Livre, l'Histoire et l'Obusier, © Rose-Hélène Ledanseur)

previous version by fastening to the waist and with a considerably shorter skirt. The front lapels that were present on the former habit were united to form a single front plastron on the habit-veste. The habit-veste retained all the colours and the basic features of the old coat. The new regulations also prescribed that the existing white waistcoat had to be replaced with a new design featuring a round-fronted shape (which was to be invisible beneath the habit-veste). Two types of breeches were issued to each dragoon: the first was made of off-white coarse hide and the second was made of canvas. The former was used on parade while the latter – being in various shades of grey and brown – was fastened from top to bottom up the sides with bone buttons (being of common use on campaign).

The trumpeters of the dragoon regiments were uniformed with habit in reversed colours, ie, they were dressed in regimental colour with dark green facings. The musicians' dress had white piping on collar, cuffs and frontal lapels. The epaulettes of trumpeters were white. The dress regulations of 1812 regularised the uniforms of the musicians, by introducing a standard Imperial livery that had to be worn by all. This consisted of a dark green single-breasted jacket ornamented with stripes of lace having alternate yellow and green segments. The yellow segments were decorated with an interwoven dark green crowned 'N', while the dark green ones were decorated with an interwoven yellow Imperial Eagle. The outfit of the dragoons was completed with tall black leather boots and white leather gauntlets.

The epaulettes of officers were silver and showed their rank. The NCOs' rank was shown by simple stripes of white cloth that were applied on the lower sleeves, while the years of service of both NCOs and rankers were shown by red inverted chevrons that were applied on the left upper sleeve. The belt equipment of all ranks was white leather. The saddlecoth consisted of a white half-shabraque made of sheepskin that was edged with small triangles of cloth in regimental colour, and of a dark green shabraque edged in white that had a white regimental number on the back corner.

Until 1804, the French dragoons were equipped with the same M1777 Charleville musket that was issued to the line infantry. In that year, however, they were re-equipped with the new cavalry musketoon of the 'Year IX' model that was designed specifically for them. This was later produced in a slightly improved version, known as the 'Year XI' model. Both the early musket and the musketoon could mount a bayonet. Each dragoon also had a couple of flintlock pistols, which could be of the 'Year IX' or 'Year XIII' model. Before 1804, the swords of the dragoons were of the heavy 'Year IV' model, which was replaced – in succession – by the newer models known as 'Year IX', 'Year XI' and 'Year XII'. This last version gradually became the definitive weapon of the dragoons.

Chapter 8

The Lancers

HISTORY AND ORGANISATION

By the outbreak of the French Revolution, three of the major European armies included some units of medium cavalry equipped with lances: the Russian Army, the Austrian Army and the Prussian Army. Since the second half of the 16th century, Poland had been the homeland of a new kind of cavalry armed with lances. Its members were known as *uhlans* and soon became the national cavalry of the Polish state in the same way that the hussars were the national cavalry of Hungary. The Polish uhlans were tactically extremely versatile and flexible. Being lightly equipped, they could easily act as explorers or skirmishers. Armed with lances, they could charge against the enemy infantry or fight large cavalry battles.

Over time, the Polish lancers became famous for their mastery of the lance, which gave them a great advantage over the enemy horsemen who were armed only with swords or sabres. A Polish uhlan could kill his cavalry opponents from a specific distance by using a weapon that was simple and cheap to produce compared with a sword or a sabre.

During the second half of the 18th century, the Polish state was partitioned between the three major military powers of eastern Europe (Russia, Austria, Prussia) and ceased to be an autonomous political entity by 1795. Following these events, the Russians, Austrians and Prussians started to recruit units of lancers from their new Polish subjects. These corps had their 'baptism of fire' during the Revolutionary Wars and performed well on several occasions.

The French also soon organised units of lancers, by recruiting large numbers of Polish political exiles who were continuing the struggle for the freedom of their country by joining the French military forces. Napoleon admired his Polish soldiers for their combat, but never considered creating new lancer units made up of French horsemen, since he considered them unfit to perform the same tactical duties as the Polish cavalrymen. During the Polish campaign of 1807 against the Russians, however, by observing the actions of the Russian lancer cavalry units, Napoleon realised that the horsemen equipped with lances had enormous potential on the battlefield. Russia, unlike Austria and Prussia, had units of lancers recruited from the Polish territories, but could also deploy massive numbers of semi-regular lancers recruited from the famous Cossacks or from the nomadic peoples living in her Asian territories.

The Cossacks were without doubt among the best light cavalrymen who fought in the Napoleonic Wars: they were ferocious, fast-moving and incredibly effective. By riding on small horses, they could move very rapidly on every kind of terrain and were able to launch surprise attacks against any possible kind of enemy. They were excellent skirmishers and skilled explorers. When needed, however, they could also pursue an enemy that was in a rout, or launch frontal charges against other cavalrymen. Their mastery in the use of the lance was impressive and no match for any opponent.

Napoleon was greatly impressed by the capabilities of the Cossacks and realised that his traditional cavalry units were unable to oppose them on the battlefield on equal terms. As a result, after years of experimentation, he created national units of lancers to counter potential confrontations with the Cossacks. The lancer regiments of the Grande Armée were organised in 1811. One year later, the French Army invaded Russia and faced hordes of Cossacks. The effective and violent attacks of the Cossacks, together with the harsh weather conditions, were one of the key factors behind Napoleon's Russian disaster. During the long retreat from Moscow, the French Army was constantly harassed by

Trooper of the Elite Company, 1st Regiment of Lancers.

the Cossack light cavalry and suffered heavy casualties due to the hit-and-run tactics employed by the Russian mounted skirmishers. The defeat suffered in Russia convinced Napoleon that the Cossacks were the best cavalrymen deployed by his enemies. As a result, during the last years of his rule, the Emperor continued to sponsor the formation of new lancer units in his armed forces. During the campaigns of 1813–14, the Cossacks played a prominent role, showing their superiority on several occasions; after having followed the French from Moscow, they finally entered Paris on their small but sturdy horses.

Light Cavalrymen-Lancers

The lancers of the French Army were created with an Imperial Decree on 18 June 1811 and were given the official denomination of *Chevau-Légers Lanciers,* or Light Cavalrymen-Lancers. They were to consist of nine regiments, which were converted from regiments already in existence:

- The 1st Regiment of Lancers was formed from the 1st Regiment of Dragoons.
- The 2nd Regiment of Lancers was formed from the 3rd Regiment of Dragoons.
- The 3rd Regiment of Lancers was formed from the 8th Regiment of Dragoons.
- The 4th Regiment of Lancers was formed from the 9th Regiment of Dragoons.
- The 5th Regiment of Lancers was formed from the 10th Regiment of Dragoons.
- The 6th Regiment of Lancers was formed from the 29th Regiment of Dragoons.
- The 7th Regiment of Lancers was formed from the 1st Lancer Regiment of the Vistula Legion.
- The 8th Regiment of Lancers was formed from the 2nd Lancer Regiment of the Vistula Legion.
- The 9th Regiment of Lancers was formed from the 30th Regiment of Mounted Chasseurs.

Most of the new lancer corps were formed by converting dragoon corps; as a result, the links existing between the dragoons and the lancers were strengthened.

The **30th Regiment of Mounted Chasseurs** had a unique history, since it was mostly made up of German soldiers. It had been created in February 1811 (a few months before becoming a lancer corps). The regiment was formed by assembling the German cavalry of the Hanoverian Legion and of a dragoon regiment raised by the independent city of Hamburg. The two regiments coming from the Polish Vistula Legion were already equipped with lances and had an excellent military reputation. At the Battle of Albuera, in May 1811, they routed an entire brigade of British infantry and captured several enemy guns. Napoleon ordered the most experienced members of the Vistula Legion's cavalry and the Imperial Guard's Polish Lancers to instruct the new units of *Chevau-Légers Lanciers*.

Once their intensive training was complete, the lancer regiments soon became one of the most important components of the French Army's cavalry. They fought with great determination during the Russian campaign – which was their baptism of fire – by launching effective counterattacks against the Cossacks. They served with valour during the campaigns of 1813–14, which ended with the fall of France and abdication of the Emperor.

With the first restoration of the Bourbons, the number of lancer regiments was reduced to six, since the three foreign units were disbanded. After Napoleon returned to France, the lancer regiments participated with distinction at the Battle of Waterloo. During that clash, they launched a deadly counterattack that almost annihilated the famous Royal Scots Greys. With the end of the Napoleonic Wars, they remained a

Trooper (left), trumpeter (centre) and officer (right) of the 1st Regiment of Lancers.

stable component of the French medium cavalry. The British – who had admired the lancers at Waterloo – introduced lancer units into their mounted corps.

The internal organisation of the lancer regiments was almost the same as for the dragoons. A single company consisted of a 1st Rank equipped with lances and of a 2nd Rank equipped only with sabres.

- The 1st Rank consisted of two sergeants, four corporals and 44 troopers.
- The 2nd Rank consisted of four corporals and 44 troopers.

These were supplemented by some supernumerary elements, who were not part of the two ranks: one sergeant-major, two sergeants, three fourriers, two trumpeters and 18 troopers (half equipped with lances, half equipped with carbines). In total, only 57 horsemen out of 125 were armed with lances inside a single company. The composition of the regimental staff matched that of the dragoon units and each regiment comprised of four squadrons with two companies each. The 1st Company of the 1st Squadron, as for the dragoon regiments, was known as Elite Company.

UNIFORMS AND EQUIPMENT

The uniform assigned to the new regiments of lancers in 1811 derived from those of the dragoons and were very similar to them (especially to the one introduced in 1812, with frontal plastron instead of the old-fashioned lapels). The headgear of the lancers was a modified version of the dragoon helmet. Where the dragoon helmet's copper crest bore a horsehair mane, the lancer helmet supported a Neo-Classical black horsehair crest; where the rear of the dragoon helmet's copper cap was simply rounded, the lancer helmet had a 'rear peak' introduced to protect the back of the neck from cuts and rain. The plume, added to the headgear on parade, could be of several colours that varied according to the regiment. Most had a plume that was red or white.

When the 1812 dress regulations prohibited the use of plumes, the lancers simply removed it from their helmets and did not replace it with the coloured discs of cloth that were officially prescribed. The fatigue cap worn on service/campaign was identical to that of the dragoons, but instead of a flaming grenade on the front, it bore two crossed lances.

In 1812, the lancers received the new dark green *pokalem*, with two crossed lances embroidered in regimental colour on the front. The soldiers of the Elite Company wore the same helmet as the other troopers, but with the horsehair crest in red. In addition, they also had red-fringed epaulettes. The regiments of lancers, unlike those of dragoons, did not include any sappers in their regimental staff. The trumpeters used the same headgear as the ordinary lancers, but with white crest and plume.

With full dress, the lancers wore a dark green *habit-veste* coat, which had a standing collar and pointed cuffs in regimental colour. Also, the frontal plastron of the coat was in regimental colour; the pointed cuffs had no cuff flaps. The frontal plastron of the habit-veste was reversible and could be buttoned back to reveal the facing colour or buttoned across to show its dark green side plus a narrow strip in regimental colour. The turn-backs of the short tails were in regimental colour like the other facings: scarlet red for the 1st Regiment, orange for the 2nd Regiment, pink for the 3rd Regiment, crimson red for the 4th Regiment, sky blue for the 5th Regiment and madder red for the 6th Regiment.

The last three regiments of lancers had specific uniforms. The turn-backs of the habit-veste were supposed to be decorated with dark green badges reproducing an Imperial Eagle; these badges, however, were quite rare to find on the actual uniforms. The buttons of the coat were yellow metal. A sleeveless and round-edged white waistcoat was worn beneath the habit-veste, being practically impossible to see.

Above left: **Trumpeter of the 1st Regiment of Lancers wearing the new Imperial livery introduced in 1812.**

Above right: **Officer of the hussars serving as 'Aide-de-camp' and wearing service dress with bicorn.**
(Photo: Le Livre, l'Histoire et l'Obusier, © Rose-Hélène Ledanseur)

For most types of duties, the full dress habit-veste described above was replaced with a dark green single-breasted shell-jacket, which had piping in regimental colour on the front and on the facings.

Trumpeters wore the same habit-veste of the ordinary lancers but with white epaulettes and white piping to the collar, cuffs and frontal plastron. In addition, they had decorative stripes of golden lace on the sleeves and on the front of their coat (which was single-breasted and thus did not have the standard frontal plastron). The dress regulations of 1812 regularised the uniforms of the musicians, by introducing the standard Imperial livery that was also prescribed for the trumpeters of the dragoon regiments.

All the lancers wore dark green Hungarian breeches on parade, which were laced down the outer leg and on the edges of the front flaps in yellow. The ornament of the flaps consisted of an inverted arrowhead device for the regiments numbered 1–4 and of a more complicated Hungarian knot for regiments numbered 5–6. On campaign, dark green overalls, reinforced with black leather on the inside, were of general use. These had side-stripes in regimental colour and yellow metal buttons applied down the outer leg. With the progression of time, especially after the Russian campaign, overalls of different colours (most notably grey ones) became increasingly popular.

The outfit of the lancers was completed by black leather Hussar boots with yellow top piping and frontal tassel, plus white leather gauntlet-like gloves.

The epaulettes of officers were golden and displayed their rank. The NCOs' rank was shown by simple stripes of yellow cloth that were applied on the lover sleeves, while the years of service of both NCOs and rankers were shown by red inverted chevrons that were applied on the left upper sleeve. The belt equipment of all ranks was white leather.

The saddlecoth consisted of a white half-shabraque made of sheepskin that was edged with small triangles of cloth in regimental colour and of a dark green shabraque edged in yellow that had a yellow regimental number on the back corner.

The main weapon of the lancers was a 275cm-long lance, which had a shaft made of hardwood (such as ash) and a point of steel. The bottom of the lance had a steel 'shoe' to protect the wood of the shaft when the weapon was resting on the ground. The centre of the shaft had a whitened leather grip and a loop for the fingers known as *martingale*. The point was made with a flattened diamond-shaped section that allowed easier penetration; it was secured by long steel straps that made it harder to chop off with a sword or sabre. The lance was decorated with a red-and-white pennon (in perfect Polish fashion). In addition to the lance, the lancers also carried a flintlock musketoon of the 'Year IX' model, a light cavalry sabre of the 'Year IX' model and a couple of flintlock pistols of the 'Year IX' or 'Year XIII' model.

The regiments numbered 7–9 had the same equipment as the other regiments, but wore specific uniforms. The two units that had previously been part of the Vistula Legion were dressed in perfect Polish style: each had a dark blue *czapka* with squared top piped in white and on the front, tricolour French cockade, white cords and flounders, brass frontal plate including a central part in white metal bearing a letter 'N', black bottom band, black peak edged in brass, brass chinscale and black plume with point in regimental colour (yellow for the 7th Regiment, red for the 8th Regiment); dark blue *kurtka* with standing collar, pointed cuffs, frontal plastron and short turn-backs in regimental colour. White epaulettes, white aiguillettes on the left shoulder. Dark blue trousers with double side-stripes in regimental colour, black leather boots and white belt equipment. The shabraque was dark blue with external edging in regimental colour.

The 9th Regiment of Lancers, formerly the 30th Regiment of Mounted Chasseurs, had the following uniform: red czapka with squared top piped in white on the edges and on the front, tricolour French cockade, white cords and flounders, brass frontal plate including a central part in white metal bearing a letter 'N', black bottom band, black peak edged in brass, brass chinscale and yellow short plume; dark green kurtka with standing collar, pointed cuffs, frontal plastron and short turn-backs in yellow. The dark green shoulder straps were piped in yellow. The red trousers had large dark green side-stripes; black leather boots and white belt equipment completed the outfit. The shabraque was red with external edging in dark green.

Chapter 9

The Hussars

HISTORY AND ORGANISATION

During the Grand Alliance War of 1688–97, which saw the Kingdom of France fighting a large military alliance that comprised Austria, England, the Netherlands and Spain, the Habsburgs deployed three regiments of Hungarian hussars against the French. These performed well and their military achievements were noticed by Louis XIV of France, persuading him to organise units of hussars inside his own military forces. France, however, did not have access to any communities of 'frontier soldiers' with the correct skill set from which a new corps could be recruited, so selected to employ foreign mercenaries for this task.

The light horsemen of the Habsburgs came from the so-called Military Frontier of Croatia and Slavonia or from the border territories of Hungary. These were experienced recruits who had spent most of their careers fighting the Turks to defend their homeland. Finding mercenaries with such military expertise was not easy for Louis XIV, but by 1692, the first hussar regiment of the French Army had been raised. This was known as *Hussards Royaux*, or Royal Hussars, and was recruited from Hungarian deserters of the Austrian Army. In 1698, however, the corps was disbanded following the end of the Grand Alliance War.

The French military authorities had seen that the hussars had great military potential, since they were capable of raiding sources of fodder and provisions during military campaigns as well as pursuing fleeing enemy troops after a victory. During the years that followed the disbandment of the *Hussards Royaux*, several new attempts were made to create a new unit of hussars inside the French Army. The Hungarian light cavalrymen used to fight in open order and were famous for being excellent marksmen. Training French horsemen to perform this way was not easy and was the main cause of the early difficulties experienced by France while attempting to raise new regiments of hussars.

In 1701, following the outbreak of the War of the Spanish Succession, the Royal Hussars Regiment was re-formed with Hungarian soldiers whose services were offered to France by Bavaria (that country was an ally of Louis XIV). In 1719, Count Berchény, a Hungarian political exile living in France, was ordered to recruit a new regiment of hussars for the French Army in the lands of the Ottoman Empire. In 1734, during the War of the Polish Succession, Count Esterhazy (another Hungarian political exile living in France) raised a third regiment of hussars in Strasbourg from deserters of the Austrian Army. During the War of the Austrian Succession (1740–48), another four regiments of hussars were created, bringing the total to seven.

Following the outbreak of the Seven Years' War in 1762, the French government consolidated the existing units of hussars into just three regiments. These gradually lost their original 'foreign' character, with new members recruited as ordinary French horsemen, and they received the same training as the original Hungarian hussars. With the end of the wars fought against the Austrian Empire, France no longer had access to significant numbers of Hungarian deserters from whom the hussars could be recruited. Several of the hussar regiments' officers, however, were Hungarian aristocrats who had rebelled against the Habsburgs during the previous decades and established themselves in France as political exiles. In 1764, a fourth regiment of hussars was created. Some years later, in 1779, three of the existing regiments were required to provide one squadron each for the formation of a fifth regiment of

Officer of the 6th Regiment of Hussars.

hussars. In addition, all the hussar corps of the French Army were put under the overall command of a superior officer known as Colonel-General of the Hussars.

In May 1780, to support the war efforts of the Thirteen Colonies that were fighting for their independence against Great Britain, France sent a large expeditionary corps to North America. This comprised a unit known as Lauzun's Legion that was mostly recruited from German, Polish and Irish mercenaries who were in search of employment in the French military. Command of the corps was given to Armand Louis de Gontaut, Duke of Lauzun, who had already served in the French Army and was an experienced officer with a very adventurous temperament.

France's Legions

During the second half of the 18th century, the French Army created several units known as legions; these were miniature armies comprising sub-units of infantry, cavalry and artillery. The basic idea behind their formation was that of having some corps act independently of the rest of the army since they comprised soldiers from every branch of service. Lauzun's Legion consisted of one company of grenadiers, one company of chasseurs, two companies of fusiliers, one company of artillery and two companies of hussars (each of these consisting of one troop equipped with lances and one troop equipped with sabres).

Once in North America, the corps fought with great determination and distinguished itself during a cavalry clash that took place at Gloucester, not far from Yorktown. Here, the hussars commanded by Lauzun defeated the famous light dragoons of Banastre Tarleton's British Legion. In June 1783, the French expeditionary corps left North America and returned home. The foot components of Lauzun's Legion were all disbanded, while the mounted ones were transformed into a new regiment of hussars of the French Army. As a result, by the outbreak of the Revolution, the French military forces comprised six hussar units.

In 1791, following the reforms of the new republican government, the traditional aristocrat-led denominations were removed and the units were given distinctive progressive numbers.

- The Berchény Regiment became the 1st Hussars.
- The Chamborant Regiment became the 2nd Hussars.
- The Conflans Regiment became the 3rd Hussars.
- The Esterhazy Regiment became the 4th Hussars.
- The Colonel-General Regiment became the 5th Hussars.
- The Lauzun Regiment became the 6th Hussars.

In 1792, the former Conflans Regiment mutinied and joined the ranks of the anti-republican military forces that were organising a counter-revolution. As a result, the number of hussar corps was briefly reduced to five and the unit number of the former Conflans Regiment was given to the former Esterhazy Regiment. The Colonel-General Regiment became the 4th Hussars, and the Lauzun Regiment became the 5th Hussars. According to the new internal structure introduced in 1786, each hussar unit consisted of four squadrons with two companies each.

During the turbulent years of the Revolutionary Wars, several new units of volunteer hussars were formed; these corps were usually made up of young volunteers who wanted to emulate the dash and the uniforms of the real hussars. They were often temporary and could be organised in many different ways. Some of them were quite large; others consisted of just a few well-to-do gentlemen from the middle classes of Paris. The new units of volunteer hussars wore colourful uniforms and bore resonant denominations such as 'Freedom Hussars' or 'Death's Head Hussars', but had little military capability compared with the regular hussars. As a result, following the end of the military crisis that culminated with the Battle of Valmy in 1792, the French authorities disbanded the volunteer hussars and employed the best of them to create regular regiments.

On 23 November 1792, the 6th Hussars and the 7th Hussars were formed, which were soon followed by the new regiments numbered 8–11 during 1793. The 12th Hussars was created in 1794 and the 13th Hussars in 1795. This corps was very short lived, disbanded in 1796. In addition to these, there was a 7th Hussars 'bis', a former volunteer corps that had been transformed into a regular unit.

Troopers of the 1st Regiment of Hussars.

As a result of the expansion of the Hussars, when Napoleon became First Consul of the Republic in 1799, the French Army comprised 13 Hussar regiments (including the 'bis' corps). During the following years, Napoleon augmented his light cavalry by organising new corps of mounted chasseurs. In 1803, three of the existing regiments of hussars were converted into dragoons: the 11th Hussars became the new 29th Regiment of Dragoons, the 12th Hussars became the new 30th Regiment of Dragoons and the 7th Hussars 'bis' became the new 28th Regiment of Dragoons. In that same year, the following internal structure was introduced for the regiments of hussars: a single unit was to consist of four squadrons with two companies each. The 1st Company of the 1st Squadron was to be known as Elite Company.

- The regimental staff of a hussar corps was to comprise one regiment commander, three squadron commanders, two adjutant-majors, one quartermaster-paymaster, one surgeon-major, two adjutant-NCOs, one veterinary officer, one trumpet-major, one blacksmith, one craftsman-saddler, one craftsman-tailor, one craftsman-cobbler and one craftsman-armourer.
- A single company consisted of one captain, one lieutenant, two second-lieutenants, one chief staff-sergeant, four staff sergeants, one brigadier-fourrier, four brigadiers, two trumpeters and 80 troopers.
- In 1806, the composition of the regimental staff was slightly changed to one colonel, one major, three squadron commanders, two adjutant-majors, one quartermaster-paymaster, one surgeon-major, one aide-surgeon, two surgeons, two adjutant-NCOs, one veterinary officer, one trumpet-brigadier, one craftsman-saddler, one craftsman-tailor, one craftsman-cobbler and one craftsman-armourer.
- The single companies adopted the following structure: one captain, one lieutenant, two second-lieutenants, one chief staff-sergeant, four staff sergeants, one brigadier-fourrier, eight brigadiers, two trumpeters and 84 troopers.

On 9 March 1809, a ninth company acting as 'depot' was added to each hussar regiment. In 1810, following the annexation of the Kingdom of Holland to the French Empire, the former 2nd Hussar Regiment of the Dutch Army became the new 11th Hussar Regiment of the French Army. In 1812, the number of squadrons in each regiment was increased to six and the depot company was disbanded.

- The composition of the regimental staff became: one colonel, one major, two squadron commanders, one quartermaster-paymaster, one surgeon-major, one aide-surgeon, two surgeons, one orderly, two adjutant-NCOs, two veterinary officers, one trumpet-brigadier, one craftsman-saddler, one craftsman-tailor, one craftsman-cobbler and one craftsman-armourer.
- The single companies adopted the following structure: one captain, one lieutenant, two second-lieutenants, one chief staff-sergeant, four staff sergeants, one brigadier-fourrier, eight brigadiers, two trumpeters, one blacksmith and 108 troopers.

In January 1812, three squadrons of the 9th Hussars that were serving in Spain were temporarily detached from their parent unit to form a new 9th Hussars 'bis'. In 1813, the detached element became the new 12th Hussar Regiment.

The last expansion of the French hussars came in 1813, following the disastrous Russian campaign, when Napoleon decided to use the conscripts from the Italian departments of Empire to create two new units of hussars. The 13th Regiment of Hussars was organised with recruits from central Italy, while the 14th Regiment of Hussars was filled with recruits from northern Italy. The 13th Hussars was dissolved on 13 December 1813 after severe losses, but was raised again in January 1814 and populated with former members of a foreign hussar unit that had recently disbanded (the Jérome-Napoléon Regiment of the Westphalian Army). The 14th Hussars was disbanded on 11 November 1813, but was soon reorganised after absorbing the former members of some cavalry units that had recently been dissolved. With the first restoration of the Bourbons in 1814, only the first six regiments of hussars were retained in service; as a result, in 1815, Napoleon fought his Belgian campaign with an insufficient number of light cavalry units.

Troopers of the 5th Regiment of Hussars.

Light Cavalry in Battle

Napoleon used his light cavalry in a very effective and innovative way during the military campaigns of 1805–15. His hussars conducted long-range reconnaissance missions but were also employed quite frequently on rear and outpost protection of the main marching columns. The Emperor showed his enemies that the light cavalry could be used also to perform defensive duties as well as offensive ones. During the Prussian campaign of 1806, Napoleon formed an independent Light Cavalry Brigade consisting of the 5th Hussars and 7th Hussars, which was put under the command of General Lasalle.

Lasalle represented the archetype of the hussar, since he had a very anarchic character and was a daring adventurer. Famed for his personal exploits, which included love affairs and many duels, Lasalle was a perfect light cavalry commander with great personal skills. During the campaign of 1806, his hussar brigade became known as the 'Brigade Infernale', or 'Hellish Brigade', since it moved very rapidly through enemy territory to gather information as well as food supplies. After the French victory at the Battle of Jena, Lasalle moved towards the enemy city of Stettin and arrived well ahead of the main French force.

Stettin was a fortified centre defended by a large garrison of more than 5,000 Prussian soldiers, who could count on 160 artillery guns of different calibre. Lasalle, pretending that the entire French Army had arrived, demanded the surrender of Stettin. The Prussian defenders of the city did not understand that the French officer and his few hussars were initiating a gigantic bluff and thus, fearing that there was no hope of escape, they surrendered without fighting. When Napoleon was informed that just two regiments of hussars (500 men in total) had captured Stettin, he wrote to Murat, 'If your Light Cavalry captures fortified towns, I'll have to discharge my Engineer Corps and have my heavy artillery melted down.'

Despite being confined, for the most part, to scouring the countryside in the vicinity of the main columns, the hussar regiments were also able to charge against the enemy infantry, if needed. When engaged on the open field by a superior enemy mounted force, the hussars were trained to form a screen of sharpshooters about the front of their regiment and to slow down the movements of their opponents by firing upon enemy officers. Napoleon's light cavalrymen were capable of maintaining surveillance of their opponents by forcing contact with the enemy and of masking the movements of their army's main columns by using feints. The *esprit de corps* of the hussar regiments was unparalleled in the French cavalry and was based on a mix of audacity and arrogance. Sometimes criticised by more traditionalist officers because of their scarce discipline, the hussars were praised by their Emperor because of their tactical creativity and incredible audacity.

UNIFORMS AND EQUIPMENT

The excesses of the French hussars were particularly evident in their colourful uniforms, which were based – like those worn by all the hussar units of the European armies – on the traditional dress of the original Hungarian hussars.

Officer (left) and trooper (right) of the 4th Regiment of Hussars. (Photo: Le Livre, l'Histoire et l'Obusier, © Rose-Hélène Ledanseur)

The egotism of the French light cavalrymen was clearly visible in their near-anarchic mode of dress, which was admired across Europe. The hussars' uniform consisted of two main elements: a short shell-jacket known as a *dolman* and a jacket slung on the left shoulder known as a *pelisse*. These were both adorned with several rows of buttons and frogging; they were worn together with tight riding breeches decorated with colourful embroidery and with calf-length boots.

The personal equipment of the hussars was very specific. It included a curved sabre with sword-knot, a black leather cartridge pouch, a barrel sash worn around the waist, short gloves and a 'sabretache'. This was a flat pouch attached to the belt of the sabre that was used to transport documents; it was strongly associated with the hussars and was decorated with rich embroidery. Unlike the other cavalry units of the French Army that had uniforms in distinctive colours (blue for the cuirassiers and green for the dragoons, for example), the hussar regiments were distinguished from one another by the different colours used for the manufacture of their dolmans/pelisses/breeches as well as by the different colours of their uniform facings. As a result, the dress worn by the French hussars during the Napoleonic Wars presented a bewildering variety.

Until 1803, the headgear of the hussars was a shako of the mirliton type, which was characterised by the presence of a *flamme*, or turban, that was wrapped around its body and of a detachable peak that was applied on its front. This early shako was 19cm tall with a 22cm diameter. It had a coloured plume and a tricolour cockade on the left side. The flamme of the mirliton was in the facing colour of each regiment, while the main body of the shako was black. Coloured cords and flounders were frequently wrapped around the headgear together with the turban. In 1803, a new model of shako was introduced after modifications were made to the original: both the flamme and the detachable peak were removed, the cockade and the plume were moved to the front of the headgear and a plate was added beneath the cockade. The brass plate was lozenge-shaped and bore the regimental number. The shako was held in place with a strap that passed beneath the wearer's chin and a cord was attached to the uniform to prevent the eventual loss of the headgear should it be toppled. During 1805–06, the shako was slightly modified in its shape, becoming taller and more bell-shaped; in addition, its strap was replaced by brass chinscales. As a result of these changes, in 1806 a new model of shako came into use. Decorative cords and flounders, although redundant, continued to be worn with this new version of the headgear.

The Elite Company of each regiment did not have shakos but black bearskin colpaks similar to busbies. These could have decorative cords and flounders like the shakos. Each colpak had a 'bag' of cloth in the same colour as the pelisse on one of its two sides (piped and tasselled in the same colour as the dolman's frogging) and a coloured plume on the front. The trumpeters of Elite Companies had white colpaks instead of the usual black ones. Over time, the use of the bearskin colpak became increasingly popular and thus, this kind of 'elite' headgear started to be worn by the officers and trumpeters of standard companies. According to the official dress regulations, however, the trumpeters of the standard companies were to use shakos in the colour of their dolman. On 9 November 1810, the use of decorative cords and flounders was officially abolished and the coloured tall plumes (which were black for most of the regiments and red for the Elite Companies) worn on the front of the headgear were replaced by a simple lentil-shaped pompom made of wool. These modifications, however, were never popular and were applied very slowly.

1812 Regulations

The new dress regulations of 1812 prohibited the use of colpaks for the Elite Companies and prescribed, instead, the use of a specific shako that was 10mm taller and wider than that worn by ordinary troopers. This elite headgear had top band, bottom band and side chevrons in red as marks of distinction. The new

Above left: Trumpeter of the 4th Regiment of Hussars; note the distinctive white busby. (Photo: Le Livre, l'Histoire et l'Obusie", © Rose-Hélène Ledanseur)

Above right: Trumpeter of the 10th Regiment of Hussars.

shako also had a different version of the frontal plate, consisting of a crescent (bearing unit number) surmounted by an Imperial Eagle; it was never popular and was adopted by just a few Elite Companies. Most preferred their colpaks. In 1812, a new informal shako was introduced for the 'centre' companies, which was known as *shako rouleau* because of its shape. This was taller than its predecessor – exceeding 20cm in height – and consisted of a reinforced black felt cylinder covered with coloured fabric. It had a black leather peak on the front and a fold-down neck cover at the rear; it had no brass plate on the front. The shako rouleau never became regulation issue, but by 1814, it had replaced the previous model of bell-shaped shako in most of the regiments.

For trumpeters, the new headgear was covered with fabric in the same colour as the pelisse. Off-duty, all hussars wore the standard bonnet de police fatigue cap in regimental colours, replaced since 1812 by the new pokalem headgear. Officers used their own versions of the headgear described above, having silver or golden top bands for the shakos and silver or golden cords and flounders for the colpaks. Off-duty, they frequently wore black bicorn hats instead of the usual fatigue caps.

Dolman and Pelisse

The dolman was fastened along its entire length by 18 half-round buttons and by their corresponding braid loops; the pelisse's loops, instead, were cut so that only the top five were long enough to be used.

Both garments had five rows of buttons on the front, but there were some regiments having only three rows. The pelisse was secured on the shoulder by a length of doubled-over cord that passed over the right shoulder and was then looped about a toggle sewn to the opposite side of the collar. The dolman had a standing collar and pointed cuffs piped in a contrasting colour; the pelisse was bordered with black fur. The front frogging of the dolman and of the pelisse was in the same colour as the collar/cuffs' piping. The pelisse had piping in this colour on its pointed cuffs.

The breeches were in the same colour as the dolman, having side-stripes and decorative embroidery on the front – known as Hungarian knots – in the same colour as the jacket's front frogging. As a result, each regiment had at least three different distinctive colours, which were used to produce the various garments according to the following scheme:

Regiment	Dolman	Collar	Cuffs	Pelisse	Breeches	Frogging
1st Hussars	Sky blue	Sky blue	Red	Sky blue	Sky blue	White
2nd Hussars	Brown	Brown	Sky blue	Brown	Sky blue	White
3rd Hussars	Grey	Grey	Red	Grey	Grey	White
4th Hussars	Dark blue	Dark blue	Red	Red	Dark blue	Yellow
5th Hussars	Sky blue	Sky blue	White	White	Sky blue	Yellow
6th Hussars	Red	Red	Red	Dark blue	Dark blue	Yellow
7th Hussars	Dark green	Red	Red	Dark green	Red	Yellow
8th Hussars	Dark green	Red	Red	Dark green	Red	White
9th Hussars	Red	Sky blue	Sky blue	Sky blue	Sky blue	Yellow
10th Hussars	Sky blue	Red	Red	Sky blue	Sky blue	White
11th Hussars	Dark blue	Red	Red	Dark blue	Dark blue	Yellow
12th Hussars	Red	Sky blue	Red	Sky blue	Sky blue	White
13th Hussars	Brown	Sky blue	Sky blue	Brown	Sky blue	White
14th Hussars	Dark green	Red	Red	Dark green	Red	White

When the frogging was white for troopers, it was silver for officers; when it was yellow for troopers, it was golden for officers. Rank was shown by inverted chevrons applied above the pointed cuffs of the dolman and pelisse; these chevrons were white or yellow for troopers/NCOs and silver or golden for officers. Years of service for troopers/NCOs were shown by inverted chevrons applied on the left sleeve of the dolman and pelisse; these chevrons were white or yellow. The Hungarian knots embroidered on the front of the breeches illustrated rank, since those of officers consisted of more stripes of lace and the number of laces corresponded to a specific rank. These decorative knots were in the same colour as the frogging and had different shapes according to each regiment. Most were simple trefoils or bastion-shaped loops.

From 1806, as an alternative to the dolman and pelisse, the hussars were given a simple single-breasted coat known as *kinski*. This had standing collar, pointed cuffs and short tails; being designed for campaign use, it was very practical to wear. The kinski was in the colour of the dolman, had collar and cuffs like those of the dolman and was piped (on the front and on the tails) in the same colour as the pelisse. The dress regulations of 1812 prescribed that a slim braid shoulder-strap was to be sewn to the left shoulder of the dolman and pelisse to secure the webbing. As an alternative to the tight Hungarian breeches, on campaign the hussars could wear comfortable overalls: these were the same colour as the breeches but opened down the side by means of 18 bone or pewter buttons along the outer seams. The inside leg and cuffs of these overalls were reinforced with black leather. The dress regulations of 1812 simplified the Hungarian knots of the breeches (ordering that they be bastion-shaped for all regiments) and also officially recognised the use of the overalls for campaign service. By 1812, they had already been modified, since they had been given a front fly concealed by a flap and now bore coloured lace or piping on the length of the outer seams.

The boots used by the hussars were of the classic Hungarian variety, with the superior edge bordered with piping and with a frontal tassel in white or yellow (silver or golden for officers). Belt equipment was white and all ranks wore wrist-length white gloves when riding.

Trumpeters were dressed as for standard hussars, but with the colpak as headgear and with all the garments having reversed colours. Quite often, the colpak and the pelisse's edging were made of white fur for musicians. The new Imperial livery introduced for all musicians since 1812 never became popular in the hussar regiments.

Curiously, some units of hussars included a squad of sappers inside their regimental staff; these elite soldiers wore the colpak instead of the shako and had a specific red badge (consisting of two crossed axes under a flaming grenade) embroidered on the sleeves of their dolman and pelisse. The sword-knot of all hussars was black leather until 1801 and later became white buff.

The *sabretache* (flat pouch) had a frontal flap bearing the regimental number encircled by a wreath of laurel leaves; there were, however, several alternative devices that usually included an Imperial Eagle. The flap of the sabretache was covered in cloth in diverse colours and was decorated with elaborately embroidered motifs. As a result, it was so valuable that a leather cover was generally slipped over it on the march or in action. A small brass shield with regimental number and Imperial Eagle was usually applied to the front of these protective covers. The 1812 regulations prescribed a general rationalisation of the sabretache's decorations, but were rarely respected by the various regiments. The barrel-sash worn by all ranks around the waist had alternating vertical bands in two colours: white/yellow (according to the colour of the frogging) and the colour of the pelisse. The saddlecoth consisted of a white or black half-shabraque made of sheepskin that was edged with small triangles of cloth in the same colour as the breeches and of a shabraque in the same colour as the breeches – edged in white/yellow for rankers/NCOs or in silver/golden for officers – that had a white/yellow or silver/golden regimental number on the back corner. Most of the superior officers had privately purchased 'exotic' shabraques obtained from the skin of a leopard or of a tiger. The external edge of the officers' shabraques consisted of a different number of stripes of lace that corresponded to a specific rank.

The main weapon of the hussars was the light cavalry sabre of the 'Year IV' model, which had curved blade and hilt/scabbard fittings made of iron. Around 1807, this started to be replaced with the new sabres of the 'Year IX' and 'Year XI' models, which had N-shaped copper basket guard and iron scabbard. Troopers also carried a flintlock musketoon, which could be of the 1786 model or, of the later 'Year IX' model. Trumpeters, NCOs and officers did not have the musketoon but carried a couple of flintlock pistols; these could be of the old 1763 model or of the newer 'Year XIII' model.

Chapter 10

The Mounted Chasseurs

HISTORY AND ORGANISATION

After the end of the War of the Austrian Succession (1740–48), most of the main European armies saw a general expansion of their light cavalry units that continued for several decades. The combat experiences of the Seven Years' War (1756–63) only confirmed the tactical importance of the new light corps. A new form of warfare was born: the *petite guerre* or little war, which was based on low-intensity combat and hit-and-run tactics.

France was one of the first European countries to understand the importance of the new light corps and thus, during the Seven Years' War, it had recruited several units of light infantry and light cavalry. These all had a temporary nature and so most of them were disbanded when the hostilities came to an end in 1763.

In 1776, the French government created a permanent corps of light troops inside its cavalry, in addition to the hussars. As a result, the existing independent units of light horsemen that had not been disbanded after 1763 were assembled to form 24 squadrons of Mounted Chasseurs. These new squadrons of light cavalry were not designed to act as independent corps since each of them was attached to a regiment of dragoons. At that time, the mounted chasseurs were still considered as an auxiliary component of the line cavalry and thus were organised in small units. Soon, however, the mounted chasseurs showed their great combat capabilities and tactical flexibility. As a result, in 1779, the 24 squadrons raised three years prior were detached from the units of dragoons and were assembled to form six independent regiments of mounted chasseurs each with four squadrons.

In 1784, the French decided to create some permanent and regular units of light infantry inside their army, following the experiences of the American Revolution. As a result, six battalions of Foot Chasseurs were organised. Each was attached to one of the existing regiments of mounted chasseurs to form new light corps with an 'experimental' nature (since each comprised four companies of foot chasseurs and four squadrons of mounted chasseurs).

In 1788, it was determined that the composite nature of the chasseur regiments was limiting for both the infantry companies and the cavalry squadrons, so the foot chasseurs were separated from the mounted chasseurs. The mounted chasseurs were reorganised into 12 regiments, numbered 1 to 12. The first six regiments were created by converting six existing dragoon corps into units of mounted chasseurs, while the remaining ones were formed by using the squadrons of mounted chasseurs that were already in existence. Each of the new units was given a specific denomination, derived from the area of France from where it was raised. Once complete, the French Army became the major military force in Europe, having the largest number of regular light cavalry corps.

The mounted chasseurs were the French equivalent of the Hungarian hussars; they performed the same tactical duties and were given light personal equipment. During the Revolutionary Wars, the number of mounted chasseur regiments was greatly expanded, with 13 new units of this kind organised during the period 1793–95. Following the military crisis of 1792, thousands of young volunteers chose to serve under the flags of the new French Republic to defend the homeland. As a result, many new units of volunteer cavalry were created across France and were sent to the front to join the regular military forces.

Above left and above right: Mounted chasseur with dolman.

The new volunteer corps of cavalry mostly had light equipment and were formed by young patriots who were full of enthusiasm but had no combat experience. As a result, their military potential could vary significantly.

Some units were well uniformed and quite numerous, others were too small and undisciplined to exist for more than a few months. From 1793, the new French government tried to rationalise the many units of volunteer light cavalry by assembling them to form some new regular corps of mounted chasseurs. In 1793, the new mounted chasseur regiments, numbered 13–24, were created by using this method, followed by the 25th Mounted Chasseurs during 1794. In 1795, however, two of the new units (the 17th and 18th) were disbanded, since their members – who were all Belgian volunteers – returned to their homeland. The regimental numbers remained vacant until the end of the Napoleonic Wars.

By the beginning of his rule as First Consul of France, Napoleon could count on 23 mounted chasseur regiments. In 1802, that figure was augmented to 24, with the creation of the new 26th Mounted Chasseurs recruited from the former members of the Piedmontese Legion's cavalry. In 1799, what remained of the Piedmontese Army had been absorbed into the French Army, since Piedmont (officially known as the Kingdom of Sardinia) was annexed to France. The Piedmontese soldiers were reorganised into two demi-brigades of line infantry, one demi-brigade of light infantry, one regiment of dragoons and one regiment of mounted chasseurs. These units, however, were quite short-lived and were all disbanded during 1802. The former Piedmontese cavalrymen were thus employed to raise the new **26th Mounted Chasseurs**.

Organisation

Each regiment of mounted chasseurs consisted of four squadrons and each of those comprised two companies. The 1st Company of the 1st Squadron, as for the hussars, was known as Elite Company. In addition to the four active squadrons, each regiment also comprised two non-combatant 'depot' squadrons. The staff of each mounted chasseur

Above left: NCO of the mounted chasseurs wearing shako with parade plume. (Photo and © Les chasseurs à cheval de la Grande Armée – 12ème Regiment)

Above right: NCO of the mounted chasseurs wearing shako with campaign protective cover. (Photo and © Les chasseurs à cheval de la Grande Armée – 12ème Régiment)

regiment consisted of the following elements: one colonel, one major, two lieutenant-colonels, one quartermaster, one surgeon-major, one chaplain, two adjutants, one trumpet-major and five master-artisans. A single company comprised the following elements: one captain, one lieutenant, one second-lieutenant, one senior staff-sergeant, four junior staff-sergeants, one fourrier, eight brigadiers, one trumpeter and 82 troopers. Each company consisted of two troops and thus had a very flexible structure.

- In 1807, the composition of the regimental staff was one colonel, one major, two squadron commanders, two adjutant-majors, one paymaster-quartermaster, one surgeon-major, one assistant-major, two sub-assistant majors, two adjutants, one trumpet-major, one veterinary surgeon and six artisans (the latter being cobblers, tailors, armourers and saddlers).

During the years 1808–11, Napoleon expanded his mounted chasseurs by raising five new regiments, numbered 27–31. Each of these had a very specific history and most were made up of non-French soldiers.

27th Mounted Chasseurs

The 27th Mounted Chasseurs was organised in September 1806 by the Duke Prosper-Louis d'Arenberg, who raised it from the Belgian territories and equipped it at his own expense. At that time, Belgium was already part of the French Empire, but the cavalry corps organised by the Duke d'Arenberg remained an autonomous unit in the early years that followed its creation. The unit bore the official denomination of *Chevau-Légers Belges du Duc d'Arenberg* or Belgian Light Cavalrymen of the Duke d'Arenberg. After reviewing the regiment, Napoleon was greatly impressed by its discipline and absorbed it into the mounted chasseurs of the French Army. As a result, on 29 May 1808, the Belgian Light Cavalrymen of the Duke d'Arenberg became the new 27th Mounted Chasseurs.

28th Mounted Chasseurs

From 1801, the Grand Duchy of Tuscany, one of the many Italian states, had been transformed by the French into a puppet realm known as the Kingdom of Etruria. It had a small army that comprised a single dragoon regiment of good quality. In December 1807, Napoleon absorbed the Kingdom of Etruria into his Empire and the small Tuscan military forces became part of the French Army. The dragoons of the Kingdom of Etruria became the 28th Mounted Chasseurs during the early months of 1808.

During the latter year, by assembling several detachments from existing regiments of mounted chasseurs deployed in Spain, three new *Régiments Provisories de Cavalerie Légère,* or Provisional Regiments of Light Cavalry, were formed. One of these, the 3rd Regiment, was transformed into a permanent corps as the **29th Mounted Chasseurs** in 1810.

The remaining two *Régiments Provisories de Cavalerie Légère* were assembled and transformed into a permanent corps as the **31st Mounted Chasseurs** in 1811. The 30th Mounted

NCO of the mounted chasseurs wearing campaign dress.
(Photo and © Les chasseurs à cheval de la Grande Armée –
12ème Régiment)

Troopers of the mounted chasseurs with M1812 uniform.

Chasseurs, instead, was formed in February 1811, by assembling the German cavalrymen of the Hanoverian Legion (see one of the next chapters for more details on this corps) and of a dragoon regiment raised by the independent city of Hamburg. As we have already seen, this unit was soon transformed into a lancer corps.

During the Napoleonic Wars, the mounted chasseurs fought with great valour, particularly during large pitched battles such as at Austerlitz. They were famed for their flexibility and were capable – if needed – of fighting on foot. Tactically, they performed the same duties as the hussars. A strong rivalry existed between the mounted chasseurs and the hussars. Frequent quarrels arose between the two on the most futile pretext.

UNIFORMS AND EQUIPMENT

Until 1803, the headgear of the mounted chasseurs was a shako of the mirliton type, which was characterised by the presence of a *flamme*, or turban, wrapped around its body, and of a detachable peak that was applied to its front. This early shako was 19cm tall and 22cm in diameter. It had a coloured plume (dark green with point in regimental colour) and a tricolour cockade on the left side. The flamme of the mirliton was in the distinctive colour of each regiment, while the main body of the shako was black. Coloured cords and flounders were frequently wrapped around the headgear together with the turban.

In 1803, a new model of shako was introduced after modifications were made to the previous one. Both the flamme and the detachable peak were removed, the cockade and the plume were moved to the front of the headgear and a plate was added beneath the cockade. The brass plate was lozenge-shaped and bore the regimental number. The shako was maintained in place by a strap that passed beneath the wearer's chin.

During 1805–06 the headgear shape was slightly modified, becoming taller and more bell-shaped; its strap was also replaced with brass chinscales. Then, in 1806, a new model of shako came into use. Decorative cords and flounders, although redundant, continued to be worn with this new version. The Elite Company of each regiment did not have shakos but black bearskin colpaks similar to busbies. These could have decorative cords and flounders like the shakos. Each colpak had a 'bag' of cloth in regimental colour on its left side that was piped and tasselled in white for NCOs/troopers, or in silver for officers. The colpak had a plume on the front, which was entirely red.

The trumpeters of Elite Companies had white colpaks instead of the usual black ones. Eventually, the bearskin colpak became increasingly popular and thus this kind of elite headgear started to be worn by the officers and trumpeters of standard companies. According to the official dress regulations, however, the trumpeters of the standard companies were to use shakos in regimental colour. On 9 November 1810, the use of decorative cords and flounders was officially abolished and the coloured tall plumes (which were dark green with point in regimental colour, or entirely red for the Elite Companies) worn on the front of the headgear were replaced by a simple lentil-shaped pompom made of wool (in regimental colour, or red for the Elite Companies). These modifications were never popular and were applied very slowly.

The new dress regulations of 1812 prohibited the use of colpaks for the Elite Companies and prescribed, instead, the use of a specific shako that was 10mm taller and wider than that worn by ordinary troopers. This elite headgear had top band, bottom band and side chevrons in red as marks of distinction. The new shako also had a different version of the frontal plate, consisting of a crescent (bearing unit number) surmounted by an Imperial Eagle. It was never popular and was adopted by just a few Elite Companies, since most preferred to retain their colpaks. Off-duty, all mounted chasseurs wore the standard *bonnet de police* fatigue cap in dark green with piping and frontal tassel in regimental colour, which was replaced from 1812 with the new pokalem headgear. Both the bonnet de police and the pokalem had the distinctive badge of the mounted chasseurs (a bugle horn) embroidered in regimental colour on the front. Officers used their own versions of the headgear described above, with silver top bands for the shakos and silver cords and flounders for the colpaks. Off-duty, they frequently wore black bicorn hats instead of the usual fatigue caps.

From their origins, the mounted chasseurs were dressed in dark green, with facings in distinctive regimental colours. During the Revolutionary Wars and up to 1806, they wore a uniform in clear hussar-style that comprised a dolman but not a pelisse. The dolman was dark green with standing collar and pointed cuffs in regimental colour. It was fastened along its entire length by 13–18 half-round pewter buttons and by their corresponding white braid loops. The jacket had three rows of buttons on the front; its collar and cuffs were piped in white. The waist, the back-seams and the front vent of the dolman were piped in white. Some regiments had dark green shoulder straps piped in white.

Above left: **NCO of the mounted chasseurs wearing campaign dress. (Photo and © Les chasseurs à cheval de la Grande Armée – 12ème Régiment)**

Above right: **NCO of the mounted chasseurs from an elite company; the busby and epaulettes are distinctive of the latter. (Photo and © Les chasseurs à cheval de la Grande Armée – 12ème Régiment)**

The jackets of the officers were identical to those of the NCOs/rankers but had five rows of buttons instead of three and the frogging/piping was silver instead of white. Rank was shown by white inverted chevrons applied above the pointed cuffs of the dolman; these chevrons were silver for officers. Years of service for troopers/NCOs were shown by white inverted chevrons applied on the left sleeve.

Trumpeters had dolmans in regimental colour with facings in dark green. Around 1806, the dolman was replaced by the so-called *habit-long*, which had been worn up to that point as campaign dress. It consisted of a long-tailed and lapelled tunic that had the same colouring as the dolman jacket except for the following. The dark green tails of the skirt were turned back to reveal the regimental colour and their turn-backs were adorned with a dark green bugle horn device; the standing collar and the pointed cuffs had piping in dark green; the frontal lapels were dark green with piping in regimental colour; the new tunic had dark green shoulder straps piped in regimental colour; on the back of the tails there were false vertical pockets that were piped in regimental colour and each featured three buttons.

The officers' rank was now shown by silver epaulettes worn on the shoulders. Under the habit-long, the mounted chasseurs wore a sleeveless waistcoat; this was single-breasted and dark green for winter and white for summer. Frequently, however, this item of dress was in regimental colour and was double-breasted instead of single-breasted. In addition, it was quite common to see waistcoats with coloured frontal frogging like the old dolmans. Trumpeters wore the habit-long with reversed colours and had white epaulettes; the mounted chasseurs of the Elite Companies, instead, had red epaulettes. From 1808, the simple single-breasted coat known as the kinski came into use. This was dark green and had a standing collar, pointed cuffs and short tails. It was designed for campaign use, and was very practical to wear. The kinski had collar and cuffs like those of the habit-long and was piped (on the front and on the tails) in regimental colour. The turn-backs of the new coat had the same bugle horn badges as the

Above left: **Trumpeter of the mounted chasseurs on foot. (Photo and © Les chasseurs à cheval de la Grande Armée – 12ème Régiment)**

Above right: **Trumpeter of the mounted chasseurs on horseback. (Photo and © Les chasseurs à cheval de la Grande Armée – 12ème Régiment)**

previous habit-long. Over time, the kinski started to be worn on all occasions except for parades (during which the habit-long continued to be used).

Trumpeters wore the kinski in regimental colour with white epaulettes, while the mounted chasseurs of the Elite Companies had red epaulettes. The dress regulations of 1812 introduced the new habit-veste that was prescribed for the dragoons and the lancers. It was basically identical to the previous kinski except for having a plastron on the front. This was dark green and piped in regimental colour. All ornaments and rank insigna remained the same as those worn on the previous habit-long and kinski. With the introduction of the new habit-veste, the trumpeters were given the new Imperial livery that has already been described for dragoons and lancers.

The mounted chasseurs wore dark green Hungarian breeches, which had side-stripes and decorative embroidery on the front – known as Hungarian knots – in regimental colour. The decorative knots had different shapes according to each regiment, but most were simple trefoils or bastion-shaped loops. They indicated rank, since those of officers consisted of more stripes of lace with the number corresponding to a specific rank.

As an alternative to the tight Hungarian breeches, on campaign, the mounted chasseurs could wear much more comfortable overalls: these were dark green and fastened down the side with 18 bone or pewter buttons along the outer seams. The inside leg and cuffs of these overalls were reinforced with black leather.

By 1812, the overalls had been modified, since they had been given a front fly concealed by a flap and now bore lace or piping in regimental colour on the length of the outer seams. Sometimes, three-pointed flaps piped in regimental colour could be attached to the front of the garment. The boots were of the classic Hungarian variety, with the superior edge bordered with piping and with a front tassel in white (silver for officers). Belt equipment was white and all ranks wore wrist-length white gloves when riding.

The saddlecoth consisted of a white half-shabraque (black for trumpeters) made of sheepskin that was edged with small triangles of cloth in regimental colour and of a dark green shabraque edged in regimental colour with regiment number in regimental colour on the back corner. Most of the senior officers had privately purchased exotic shabraques obtained from the skin of a leopard or of a tiger. The external edge of the officers' shabraques consisted of a different number of stripes of lace that corresponded to a specific rank.

The main weapon of the mounted chasseurs was the light cavalry sabre of the 'Year IV' model, which had curved blade and hilt/scabbard fittings made of iron. Around 1807, this started to be replaced with the new sabres of the 'Year IX' and 'Year XI' models, which had an N-shaped copper basket guard and iron scabbard. Troopers and NCOs also carried a flintlock musketoon, which could be of the 1786 model, or of the later 'Year IX' model. Trumpeters and officers did not have the musketoon but carried a couple of flintlock pistols that could be of the old 1763 model or of the newer 'Year XIII' model.

Chapter 11

The Artillery

HISTORY AND ORGANISATION

By the end of the 18th century, the artillery was the best in terms of quantity and quality. In 1765, it had been reformed and modernised by an extremely competent officer: Lieutenant General Jean-Baptiste Vaquette de Gribeauval. He created a brand new artillery system that introduced lighter guns of more uniform calibre, which soon became known as Gribeauval System. The new artillery pieces were a key factor in the victories of the French Army of the Revolutionary and Napoleonic periods. They were the most technologically advanced products that the French military apparatus was able to produce. Employed by competent and brilliant young officers such as Napoleon, these weapons could not be matched by other European armies. The central decades of the 18th century saw the development of mobile field artillery, since ballistics engineers and metallurgy technicians progressively lowered the weight of the gun tubes and designed lighter gun carriages. Calibres started to be standardised in order to ease logistical problems and new tactical plans regarding the use of artillery on the battlefield were designed.

Gribeauval System

The guns of the 18th century were made of bronze – an alloy of 10 parts copper to one part tin – and their methods of construction were constantly improved. Until 1750, cannons were cast hollow around a core and the core was often moved within the mould, producing an imperfect bore. This problem was solved when the Dutch began casting their guns as a single solid block and then drilling the bore on a large machine designed for this specific task. Very soon all the European armies adopted this new construction system, which had advantages. The new pieces had a better aligned bore and tighter tolerances had inferior windage – meaning, the gap between the cannonball and the bore – and thus less gas pressure escaped so that smaller gunpowder charges could hurl a projectile farther and more accurately than before. As a result, cannon barrels were thinner, shorter and lighter.

Before 1765, France possessed the only unified range of artillery in Europe, which was known as the Vallière System after the name of its creator, who standardised guns from 4-pounders through 24-pounders. Initially, some traditionalists opposed the introduction of the new Gribeauval System, and the new artillery only became fully operative in 1776. Ultimately, however, the whole French artillery was re-equipped with the newer, lighter pieces. The guns were approximately half the weight of those designed by Vallière but had the same range.

The Gribeauval System prescribed the use of three different cannons: 12-, 8- and 4-pounder, and one 6-inch howitzer for field artillery. These all had new standardised carriages, built with interchangeable parts, which were lighter and narrower than the previous ones. The carriages had two positions for the trunnions: a forward position for firing and a rear position for travelling. The draft horses started to be harnessed in pairs rather than single file, so with double the power, heavier pieces could be used. All the pieces were fitted with a rear-calibrated gunsight as well as with an elevating screw improving precision, particularly with distant targets.

The new quick-match tubes introduced by Gribeauval generated a better ignition of the gunpowder charges, which started to be placed inside pre-packaged flannel bags. A new vent-pricker, a special tool

Above left: Officer of the foot artillery with bicorn.
(Photo: Le Livre, l'Histoire et l'Obusier, © Rose-Hélène Ledanseur)

Above right: Officer of the foot artillery with pre-1812 uniform.

used to make a hole in the gunpowder bags, also came into use. For siege and garrison artillery, Gribeauval retained the calibres introduced by Vallière in 1732 but improved the pieces. Four kinds of guns were used by the French siege and garrison artillery: 24-, 16, 12- and 8-pounder siege cannons. Gribeauval also designed a range of mortars, which were mostly used for bombarding static positions: 12-inch, short 10-inch, long 10-inch, and 8-inch mortar. Napoleon replaced the 4- and 8-pounder cannons with the new 6-pounder 'Year XI' field gun. The 6-inch howitzer was replaced with the new 'Year XI' 24-pounder howitzer.

Prior to the outbreak of the Revolution, the French artillery had competent officers who for the most part were not aristocratic and so had earned their promotions. These men, including the young Napoleon, underwent a modern training that made them capable of using the pieces of the Gribeauval System in a very effective way. The artillery officers had scientific and technological skills that were unparalleled in the French Army, since they spent several years studying the latest improvements in artillery. Artillery, in practice, was the most modern and least aristocratic of the French Army's branches of service. As a result, when many royalist officers left the French military units after the outbreak of the Revolution, it was not seriously damaged, unlike the infantry or the cavalry.

Regiments

In 1791, the French artillery consisted of seven foot regiments, each of which comprised two battalions with ten companies/batteries each. During the turbulent years of the Revolutionary Wars, several units of volunteer or National Guard artillery were formed. These were made up of inexperienced soldiers who were not capable of manning their pieces in an effective way. As a result, in 1796, the French authorities disbanded all the volunteer/National Guard artillery units and used the best members to form a new regiment of regular foot artillery. Meanwhile, as with other European armies, came the development of the new horse artillery that could be created around the lighter guns designed by Gribeauval.

The first two horse or 'flying' batteries of the French Army were organised, in 1791, by General Mathieu Dumas. These had their gunners still riding on caissons and not on horses. In April

1792, nine companies of horse artillery were formed, three of which were fully mounted on horses. Recruited from the foot artillery and from the infantry grenadiers, these were not made up of expert horsemen but soon became famous for their combat capabilities. Each of these early mounted artillery companies comprised four officers, 11 NCOs, three artificers, two trumpeters and 60 gunners. In February 1794, following the success of the early 'flying companies', the mounted artillery was enlarged to comprise nine regiments (later reduced to eight) with six companies/batteries each. The new units were mostly recruited from cavalrymen, who had limited artillery skills but lots of enthusiasm.

By the end of 1799, when Napoleon became First Consul, the artillery of the French Army comprised eight foot regiments with 20 companies each and eight horse regiments with six companies each. These were supplemented by an Artillery General Staff consisting of 266 officers, 12 companies of *ouvriers* or artillery workers, and two pontoon battalions. In 1801, the number of horse artillery regiments was reduced to six and that of the artillery workers' companies was increased to 15.

- A single company/battery of foot artillery consisted of one first captain, one second captain, one first lieutenant, one second lieutenant, one sergeant-major, four sergeants, one fourrier, four corporals, two drummers, 21 workers/artificers and 77 gunners (later reduced to 68).
- A single company/battery of horse artillery comprised one first captain, one second captain, one first lieutenant, one second lieutenant, one sergeant-major, four sergeants, one fourrier, four corporals, two trumpeters, eight workers/artificers and 59 gunners.

Throughout the period taken into account, it was usual for each foot company to have six cannons and two howitzers and for each horse company to have four guns (usually 6-pounders) and two howitzers. Each single battery was a self-contained entity having its own train and thus could serve independently. In 1810, following the disbanding of the Dutch Army, a new regiment of foot artillery and a new regiment of horse artillery were organised with former members of the Dutch artillery; the mounted unit, however, was soon dissolved.

From 1811, the number of companies in each foot regiment was progressively enlarged, reaching 28 by 1813. Each of the horse regiments, instead, received an additional depot company from 1809. In addition to the foot artillery and horse artillery regiments, there were also the armourers (one company in 1803, increased to two in 1805) and the *ouvriers* who were structured on 18 companies by 1813.

- A single company of armourers consisted of four officers and 68 privates, while a company of artillery workers comprised 5 officers and 149 privates.

With the first restoration of the Bourbons in 1814, the foot artillery was reduced to eight regiments with 16 companies each and the horse artillery to four regiments with four companies each. In addition to these there were 12 companies of ouvriers and a pontoon battalion.

Drivers and Artillery Train

Initially the foot artillery relied upon civilian transport drivers hired from private contractors for moving its guns. Though they were exposed to the dangers of the battlefield, they were not subject to military discipline and were usually neglected by their employers. In 1800, Napoleon militarised the role, recruiting soldiers as drivers. This had very positive consequences. Instead of being unharnessed at the edge of the battlefield and dragged into action by the gunners, the pieces were now positioned at the heart of the action by the artillery drivers.

In 1800, eight battalions of Artillery Train were formed, one for each of the existing foot artillery regiments. These consisted of one elite and four line companies for each of the eight battalions.

- A single company comprised seven NCOs and 60 privates.

The soldiers of the train were distributed among the artillery batteries and had no officers, since they were commanded by the battery officers. In 1801, the elite company was abolished and the number of companies in each battalion was increased to six. By 1808, there were 13 battalions of the Artillery Train; in 1810 these were doubled with the formation of 'bis' units and a 14th Battalion was raised from former members of the Dutch Army. With the restoration of 1814, the Artillery Train was reorganised on four squadrons with 15 officers and 271 men each; these were increased to eight by Napoleon for the Belgian campaign of 1815.

Regimental artillery, or battalion guns, were a common feature in the late 18th century, since it was common practice to include some artillery pieces inside the line infantry units. These light guns, crewed by infantrymen, were tasked with providing immediate fire support for the foot regiments/battalions. The French line infantry included some light pieces until January 1798, when these were abolished. In June 1809, the Emperor, having at his disposal large amounts of captured guns taken from defeated enemies, reintroduced the concept of regimental artillery and assigned two light cannons plus a platoon of 22 gunners and two platoons of 20 artillery drivers to several of his line/light infantry regiments. This regimental artillery was destroyed during the Russian campaign.

Artillery Types

In addition to the foot artillery and horse artillery, the French Army also included another three categories of artillery: the **Coast Artillery**, the **Garrison Artillery** and the **Veteran Artillery**. The first was tasked with manning the shore fortifications of France and consisted of 100 independent companies of *Canonniers-Gardes-Cotes*. These were gradually expanded by Napoleon, reaching a total of 144 by 1812. Upon the first restoration of the Bourbons, the Canonniers-Gardes-Cotes were disbanded.

The Garrison Artillery was tasked with manning the many fortifications that were located on French territory and consisted of 28 independent companies of *Canonniers Sédentaires* (augmented to 30 by 1812).

The Veteran Artillery was part of a larger corps formed in 1792 and known as Invalid Companies, which was made up of old soldiers who were no longer able to perform active duties. In 1799, the Veteran Artillery included inside the Invalid Companies consisted of 13 independent companies with 52 gunners each. By 1812, there were 19 companies of Veteran Artillery; these were reduced to 10 with the first restoration of the Bourbons.

UNIFORMS AND EQUIPMENT

The French foot artillery dressed in a similar way to the line infantry and its uniforms remained almost unchanged until 1812. Being dark blue with red facings, they were very easy to recognise on the battlefield. In 1799, the foot artillery's uniform was: black bicorn with national cockade having orange-yellow lace holder and red pompom made of wool. Each wore a dark blue long-tailed coat with brass buttons and dark blue front lapels piped in red. They featured dark blue shoulder straps piped in red, dark blue collar piped in red, red round cuffs, dark blue cuff flaps piped in red, red turn-backs adorned with dark blue flaming grenade badges, horizontal pocket flaps on the back of the tails piped in red decorated with three buttons, dark blue waistcoat, dark blue trousers, black gaiters during cold months or white gaiters during hot months and black shoes.

Over time, a few features of the uniform were modified: the tails of the coat became shorter in order to be more practical and the frontal lapels started to have an accentuated curve. The black bicorn hat was worn in two different positions according to the activities that its wearer was performing: when worn across the head (*en bataille*) its wearer was ready to fight; when worn fore-and-aft (*en colonne*) its wearer was marching.

The foot artillerymen could use the bonnet de police undress cap as an alternative to the bicorn. This was dark blue with red piping and had a tasselled stocking end folded up and tucked behind the right-hand side of a stiffened headband. The tassel was red and on the front of the cap there was a red flaming grenade. According to the egalitarian principles of the Revolution, officers were dressed exactly like their men, but their uniforms were of finer material. The lace holder of the bicorn's cockade

Above left: Officer of the foot artillery with shako. (Photo: Le Livre, l'Histoire et l'Obusier, © Rose-Hélène Ledanseur)

Above right: NCO of the foot artillery. (Photo and © Pascal Thonon)

was golden for officers. In addition, officers wore a gilt gorget under their neck. This was mostly used on parade and incorporated a decorative silver device that included a flaming grenade placed above two crossed cannons. The gorget was the last remnant of the medieval knight's armour, a symbol of high military status.

An officer's rank was indicated on the uniform with gold lace epaulettes worn on the shoulders. These were designed according to a general scheme that had been introduced in 1786 and remained valid after the outbreak of the Revolution. NCOs' ranks were shown by diagonal bars of lace that were applied on the lower sleeves: two orange-yellow bars for corporals, one golden bar piped in red for sergeants and two golden bars piped in red for sergeant-majors.

Both NCOs and rankers had lace service chevrons on the left upper sleeves of their coats; these were worn point uppermost and were golden for senior NCOs or red for junior NCOs and rankers. The number of inverted chevrons corresponded to the years of service: one for ten years of service, two for 15 years and three for 20 years.

In February 1806, there was a very important modification to the uniforms of the French foot artillery, when the bicorn was replaced with a shako. The shako was made of black felt or board, which widened slightly towards the top, and had a waterproof crown. Around the top and the bottom of the shako were leather bands to reinforce its shape; and on the front was a leather peak. A leather chevron was usually applied as strengthening on each side. On the front of the top band was a tricolour cockade placed above a lozenge-shaped brass plate that bore an embossed Imperial Eagle placed above two crossed cannons and a regimental number.

The shako was kept in position by brass chinscales that consisted of circular bosses. The first boss on each side, applied on the bottom band of the headgear, was larger than the others and bore a decorative badge (a flaming grenade). Above the cockade, there was a red woollen pompom, which could be surmounted by a red plume with parade dress. Wrapped around the shako, there were red decorative cords and flounders, which were usually removed while on campaign. The shakos of the officers had gold lace on the top band, golden cords/flounders, golden lace holder for the cockade and gilded fittings.

Bardin's Regulations

On 19 January 1812, new dress regulations were promulgated for the French Army; these remained in use until the fall of Napoleon in 1815, and were named after Major Bardin, who was responsible for their issue. They retained the general features and colours of the foot artillery uniform used up to that time, but introduced some important modifications. The old coat was replaced with a double-breasted and short-tailed dark blue jacket known as habit-veste. It had dark blue plastron-style lapels piped in red on the front and vertical pockets on the back. Rank distinctions and service chevrons remained unchanged. The dark blue waistcoat, which was no longer visible, now had a lower collar and coloured shoulder straps. The black or white gaiters no longer extended over the knee. The 1812 dress regulations also introduced a new model of shako, bore a crowned Imperial Eagle atop a semi-circular plate into which the regimental number was cut. The new shako had decorative brass finials that reproduced a flaming grenade. The usual tricolour cockade and brass chinscales of the previous model of shako were retained. Cords and flounders were officially abolished, but in practice they continued to be worn by most of the regiments. The new shako had a red tufted pompom on the front. The Bardin Regulations introduced a new model of fatigue cap that replaced the previous bonnet de police known as the pokalem. It was a pie-shaped dark blue cap with a folding neck-flap that could be fastened under the chin. The pokalem was piped in red and bore a red flaming grenade on the front.

The uniforms of the foot artillery musicians were governed, until the promulgation of the 1812 dress regulations, by the personal tastes of

Above left: Foot artilleryman of the Imperial Guard wearing winter great coat and bonnet de police. (Photo: Le Livre, l'Histoire et l'Obusier, © Rose-Hélène Ledanseur)

Above right: Gunner of the foot artillery wearing campaign blouse and bonnet de police. (Photo: Le Livre, l'Histoire et l'Obusier, © Rose-Hélène Ledanseur)

the colonels commanding the single regiments. The members of the regimental band wore coats in extravagant colours (red in most cases), which sometimes had an exotic appearance. They were frequently used together with non-regulation headgear such as the bicorn hat adorned with ostrich-feathers, or the Polish czapkas. The uniforms of the regimental bandsmen were a triumph of colours: their facings were all trimmed with multi-colour lace, they had trefoil-shaped epaulettes in the same colour as their trimming and sometimes included decorative shoulder wings. Their trousers could be decorated on the front with embroidered knots, while the standard leg-wear was usually replaced with black leather half-boots incorporating coloured top edging and frontal tassel. Plumes, pompoms, cords and flounders of the shakos could be in many different colours (usually matching the coat or its trimming).

The musicians of the single companies/batteries were dressed in a much simpler way and looked more or less like their comrades. They had coloured lacing on the facings, on the pockets and on the turn-backs; in addition, they usually had decorative stripes of coloured lace applied on the sleeves and coloured shoulder-wings. Shako ornaments, company distinctions, badges on the turn-backs and epaulettes were all the same as those of the standard gunners. The Bardin Regulations were an attempt to regularise the uniforms by introducing a standard Imperial livery. It consisted of a dark green single-breasted jacket decorated with stripes of lace with alternate yellow and green segments. The yellow segments were decorated with an interwoven dark green crowned 'N', while the dark green segments were decorated with an interwoven yellow Imperial Eagle. During the brief restoration of the Bourbons in 1814, some elements of the foot artillery uniform were modified: the tricolour cockade was replaced with the royal white one and a new shako plate bearing the coat-of-arms of the royal family came into use.

Horse Artillery Uniforms

The French horse artillery was always dressed in a similar way to the cavalry's mounted chasseurs, but in dark blue with red facings. Until 1803, the headgear of the mounted artillery was a shako of the mirliton type, which was characterised by the presence of a flamme, or turban, that was wrapped around its body, and of a detachable peak that was applied on its front. This early shako was 19cm tall and 22cm in diameter. It had a red plume and a tricolour cockade on the left side. The flamme of the mirliton was red, while the main body of the shako was black. Red cords and flounders were frequently wrapped around the headgear together with the turban. In 1803, a new model of shako was introduced after modifications were made to the previous one. Both the flamme and the detachable peak were removed, the cockade and the plume were moved to the front of the headgear and a plate was added beneath the cockade. The brass plate was lozenge-shaped and bore the regimental number together with two crossed cannons. The shako was maintained with a strap that passed beneath the wearer's chin.

During 1805–06, the headgear was modified, becoming taller and more bell-shaped. In addition, its strap was replaced by brass chinscales. As a result of these changes, in 1806, a new model of shako came into use. Decorative cords and flounders, although redundant, continued to be worn with this new version of the headgear. On 9 November 1810, the use of decorative cords and flounders was officially abolished and the red plume worn on the front of the headgear was replaced by a simple lentil-shaped pompom made of wool. These modifications, however, never became particularly popular and thus were applied very slowly. Like the mounted chasseurs, officers and trumpeters frequently had a black colpak with red plume and bag instead of the standard shako.

The new shako, introduced in 1812 for the foot artillery, was also given to the horse artillery. This had a frontal plate consisting of a crescent (bearing unit number) surmounted by an Imperial Eagle. Off-duty, all horse artillerymen wore the standard bonnet de police fatigue cap in dark blue with piping and frontal tassel in red, which was replaced from 1812 by the new pokalem headgear. Both the bonnet de police and the pokalem had the distinctive flaming grenade of the artillery embroidered in red on the front. Officers

Trumpeter (left) and troopers (right) of the mounted artillery wearing busby and dolman.

used their own versions of the headgears described above, having golden top bands for the shakos and golden cords and flounders for the colpaks.

Up to 1811, the mounted artillerymen wore a uniform in clear hussar-style that comprised a dolman but not a pelisse. The dolman was dark blue with standing collar piped in red, with red pointed cuffs. It was fastened along its entire length by 13–18 half-round pewter buttons and by their corresponding red braid loops. The jacket had three rows of buttons on the front; its waist, back-seams and front vent were piped in red. The jackets of the officers were identical to those of the NCOs/rankers but had five rows of buttons instead of three and their frogging/piping was golden instead of red.

Above left: Officer of the mounted artillery wearing shako and dolman.

Above right: Troopers of the mounted artillery wearing pre-1812 shako and habit-long.

Rank was shown by yellow inverted chevrons applied above the pointed cuffs of the dolman; these chevrons were golden for officers. Years of service for troopers/NCOs were indicated by red inverted chevrons applied on the left sleeve. Trumpeters had dolmans in red with facings in dark blue. In 1811, the dolman was replaced by the *habit-long*, which had been worn until then as campaign dress. This consisted of a long-tailed tunic with lapels that had the same colouring as the dolman jacket, except that the dark blue tails of the skirt were turned back to reveal their red lining and their turn-backs were adorned with a dark blue flaming grenade device. The front lapels were dark blue with red piping. The new tunic had red epaulettes. On the back of the tails, there were false vertical pockets that were piped in red and featured three buttons each.

The officers' rank was now shown by golden epaulettes worn on the shoulders. Under the habit-long, the mounted artillerymen wore a sleeveless waistcoat; this was single-breasted and dark blue. Frequently, however, this item of dress was red and was double-breasted instead of single-breasted. The waistcoat had red coloured frontal frogging like the old dolman. Trumpeters wore the habit-long with reversed colours and had white epaulettes.

From 1811, the single-breasted coat, known as *kinski*, came into use for campaign dress. This was dark blue and had standing collar, pointed cuffs and short tails; being designed for campaign use, it was very

***Above left**: Officer of the coastal artillery. Photo: Le Livre, l'Histoire et l'Obusier", © Rose-Hélène Ledanseur)*

***Above middle**: Private of the Artillery Train of the Imperial Guard. (Photo: Le Livre, l'Histoire et l'Obusier, © Rose-Hélène Ledanseur*

***Above right**: Private of the Artillery Train of the Imperial Guard, wearing winter dress. (Photo: Le Livre, l'Histoire et l'Obusier, © Rose-Hélène Ledanseur)*

practical to wear. The kinski had collar and cuffs like those of the habit-long and was piped (on the front and on the tails) in red. The turn-backs of the new coat had the same flaming grenade badges of the previous habit-long. Ultimately, the kinski started to be worn on all occasions except for parades (during which the habit-long continued to be used).

Trumpeters wore the kinski in red and had white epaulettes. The dress regulations of 1812 introduced the new habit-veste that was prescribed for the foot artillery; it was basically identical to the previous kinski except for having a plastron on the front. This was dark blue and was piped in red. All ornaments and rank insignia remained the same as those worn on the previous habit-long. With the introduction of the new habit-veste the trumpeters were given the new Imperial livery that has already been described for foot artillery.

The horse artillerymen wore dark blue Hungarian breeches, incorporating side-stripes and decorative embroidery on the front – known as Hungarian knots – in red. The decorative knots were trefoil-shaped until 1812 and then bastion-shaped; they denoted rank, since those of officers consisted of more stripes of lace and the number of stripes corresponded to a specific rank. As an alternative to the tight Hungarian breeches, on campaign the mounted artillerymen could wear comfortable overalls. These were dark blue and opened by means of 18 bone or pewter buttons along the outer seams. The inside leg and cuffs of these overalls were reinforced with black leather. By 1812, the overalls had been modified, since they had been given a front fly concealed by a flap and now bore lace or piping in red on the length of the outer seams. Sometimes three-pointed flaps piped in red could be attached to the front of the garment.

The boots used by the horse artillerymen were of the classic Hungarian variety, with the superior edge bordered with piping and with a frontal tassel in yellow (golden for officers). Belt equipment was white and all ranks wore wrist-length white gloves when riding.

The saddlecoth consisted of a white half-shabraque (black for trumpeters) made of sheepskin edged with small triangles of red cloth and of a dark blue shabraque edged in red that had a red flaming grenade on the back corner. Most of the senior officers had exotic shabraques obtained from the skin of a leopard/tiger. The external edge of the officers' shabraques consisted of a different number of stripes of lace that corresponded to a specific rank. Like the hussars, the horse artillerymen had *sabretache* and barrel-sash in dark blue and red.

The *ouvriers,* or artillery workers, armourers and pontoniers, were dressed exactly like the foot artillerymen. The Garrison Artillery and the Veteran Artillery had the same uniform as the foot artillery.

The *Cannoniers-Gardes-Cotes* had a specific uniform. Until 1810, they wore black bicorn with tricolour national cockade having orange-yellow lace holder, red pompom and red tuft; white coat with medium blue collar, round cuffs, cuff flaps, frontal lapels and turn-backs; red epaulettes, white waistcoat, white trousers, black gaiters and black shoes.

1810 Uniform

In 1810, the following new uniform was introduced: black shako with tricolour national cockade, red pompom, red tuft and brass frontal plate showing an anchor over two crossed cannons; dark blue coat with green collar, round cuffs, cuff flaps, frontal lapels and turn-backs; red epaulettes, green waistcoat, green trousers, black stockings and black shoes. On the turn-backs of the coat there were decorative flaming grenade badges, in medium blue for the first model of coat and in dark blue for the second model introduced in 1810.

The first uniform given to the Artillery Train was as follows: black bicorn with tricolour national cockade having orange-yellow lace holder and coloured tuft (half iron-grey and half red), iron-grey coat with dark blue collar, round cuffs, front lapels and turn-backs; iron grey shoulder straps piped in dark blue, white waistcoat, white breeches and black boots. In 1807, the bicorn was replaced with the shako, and in 1808 the main colour of the uniform was changed. As a result, the new dress of the Artillery Train was: black shako with sky-blue frontal plume, cords and flounders; tricolour national cockade with sky-blue lace holder, sky-blue pompom with red central part bearing unit number in white metal, white metal chinscale and white metal frontal plate bearing an Imperial Eagle above the unit number; sky-blue coat with dark blue collar, round cuffs and front lapels piped in sky-blue, sky-blue cuff flaps piped in dark blue, dark blue turn-backs, sky-blue shoulder straps piped in dark blue, sky-blue waistcoat, white breeches and black leather boots.

The new sky-blue colour of the tunic, in most cases, was practically identical to the previous iron-grey. In 1810, the coat was replaced with a simpler single-breasted *surtout* of the same colour, having dark blue collar, cuffs and turn-backs all piped in white. This was usually worn together with sky-blue overalls incorporating side buttons and leather reinforcements, which were popular since the creation of the Artillery Train. In 1812, they were also given the new habit-veste – in iron-grey – and the new brass plate for the shako; as a result, the uniform of the Artillery Train became as follows: black shako with tricolour national cockade, red pompom, white metal chinscale and white metal frontal plate bearing an Imperial Eagle above a crescent with unit number; iron grey habit-veste with dark blue collar, round cuffs, frontal plastron and short turn-backs, iron grey cuff flaps and shoulder straps piped in dark blue, iron grey flaming grenade badges on the turn-backs, white breeches or iron grey overalls, and black leather boots.

Until 1812, the musicians of the Artillery Train were dressed with uniforms featuring reversed colours; with the new dress regulations of that year, they were given the Imperial livery. Belt equipment was white and all ranks wore white leather gauntlet-like gloves. The saddlecoth consisted of a white half-shabraque made of sheepskin that was edged with small triangles of dark blue cloth, plus an iron grey shabraque edged in white that had a white flaming grenade on the back corner.

Chapter 12

Technical Corps

HISTORY AND ORGANISATION

In 1789, the French Army comprised a small staff of engineer officers plus six companies of sappers and six companies of miners. The companies of miners were numerically small, not particularly regarded and were part – at least formally – of the artillery.

The engineer officers were extremely competent and came from middle-class families; they did not suffer from the outbreak of the Revolution and from the subsequent exile of the aristocratic officers. In 1793, the new republican government assembled the engineer officers, the miners and the sappers into an independent Engineer Corps; the miners continued to consist of six companies, while the sappers were increased to nine battalions with eight companies in each. In 1798, the sappers were reduced to four battalions and later, during 1799, to just two battalions with 1,800 men in each.

A single company of sappers comprised four officers, nine NCOs, four artisans, one drummer and 48 privates. By 1806, the number of privates had increased to 154. During that same year, the Engineer Train was established, which was organised as a single battalion with seven companies in 1811. In 1808, the miners were restructured on two battalions with five companies each (later increased to six); in 1811, instead, an independent company of engineer workers (*ouvriers*) was formed. Meanwhile, the number of sapper battalions was progressively expanded so that by 1812 there were a total of eight units. From 1809, the staff of engineer officers was supplemented by a small corps of Geographical Engineers, consisting of 90 officers who were tasked with producing accurate maps for the army. The French sappers were supported in their activities by several labour battalions recruited from POWs, which were rarely employed on the battlefield. These were the following: *Compagnies de Pionniers*, independent companies formed from conscripts who had mutilated themselves to avoid military service; *Pionniers Blancs*, two battalions formed from POWs; and *Pionniers Espagnols*, four companies formed from Spanish POWs interned in France after their country left the alliance with Napoleon to side with Great Britain.

During the first years of the Napoleonic period, all the materiel of the French Army were transported by civilian contractors; the Emperor, however, was never particularly happy with the services provided, since corruption was rife. In 1807, Napoleon militarised the civilian transporters to create the so-called Train of the Equipment. This initially consisted of eight battalions with four companies each, a single battalion being equipped with 140 wagons. Four wagons in each company were used as ambulances, while the remainder were allocated either to individual units to carry their provisions or to a centralised train that was tasked with transporting reserve rations/munitions. In time, the Train of the Equipment was greatly expanded, reaching an establishment with 21 battalions by 1812. One of these consisted entirely of medical vehicles. After the Russian campaign, the number of battalions was temporarily reduced to nine but later increased to 12.

- Each battalion of the Train of the Equipment had a staff comprising four officers, five NCOs and five craftsmen.
- A single company consisted of one sub-lieutenant, seven NCOs, four craftsmen and 80 drivers.
- From 1812, the Train of the Equipment also comprised two battalions of workers or ouvriers.

UNIFORMS AND EQUIPMENT

The French engineer officers, sappers and miners were always dressed like the foot artillery but with facings in black. In 1799, their uniform was: black bicorn with national cockade having orange-yellow lace holder and red pompom made of wool (this was half-red and half-black for miners), dark blue long-tailed coat with brass buttons and black front lapels piped in red, dark blue shoulder straps piped in red, black collar piped in red, black round cuffs piped in red, black cuff flaps piped in red, red turn-backs adorned with dark blue flaming grenade badges, horizontal pocket flaps on the back of the tails piped in red and three decorative buttons on each. The outfit was complete with dark blue waistcoat, dark blue trousers, black gaiters for cold months or white gaiters for hot months and black shoes. Later, a few features of the uniform were modified. The tails of the coat became shorter in order to be more practical and the front lapels started to have an accentuated curve.

As an alternative to the bicorn, all engineers could use the bonnet de police undress cap. It was dark blue with red piping and had a tasselled stocking end folded up and tucked behind the right-hand side of a stiffened headband. The tassel was red, and on the front of the cap was a red badge consisting of two crossed axes. Officers were dressed exactly like their men, but their uniforms were of finer material. The lace holder of the bicorn's cockade was golden for officers. In addition, they wore a gilt gorget under their neck. This was mostly used on parade and incorporated a decorative silver device that included two crossed axes.

Above left: **Private of the Artillery Train with M1812 dress and bonnet de police fatigue cap.**

Above right: **Drummer of the engineers with pre-1812 dress.**

Officer rank was depicted on the uniform via gold lace epaulettes that were worn on the shoulders.

NCOs' ranks were shown by diagonal bars of lace that were applied on the lower sleeves: two orange-yellow bars for corporals, one golden bar piped in red for sergeants, two golden bars piped in red for sergeant-majors. Both NCOs and rankers had lace service chevrons on the left upper sleeves of their coats; these were worn point uppermost and were golden for senior NCOs or red for junior NCOs and rankers.

In 1806, the bicorn was replaced with the shako. The shako was made of black felt or board, which widened slightly towards the top and had a waterproof crown. Around the top and the bottom of the shako there were leather bands in red that reinforced it; on the front there was a leather peak. A red leather chevron was applied as strengthening on each side of the headgear. On the front of the top band there was a tricolour cockade placed above a lozenge-shaped brass plate that bore an embossed Imperial Eagle placed above a unit number. The shako was kept in position by brass chinscales that consisted of circular bosses; the first boss on each side, applied on the bottom band of the headgear, was larger than the others. Above the cockade there was a red woollen pompom (half-red and half-black for miners), surmounted by a small tuft of the same colour. Wrapped around the shako, there were red decorative cords and flounders, which were usually removed while on campaign. Officer shakos had gold lace on the top band, golden cords/flounders, golden lace holder for the cockade and gilded fittings.

1812 Regulations

The new dress regulations of 1812 retained the general features and colours of the engineer uniform used up to that time, but introduced some important modifications. The old coat was replaced with a double-breasted and short-tailed dark blue jacket known as the habit-veste. This jacket had black plastron-style lapels piped in red on the front and vertical pockets on the back. Rank distinctions and service chevrons remained unchanged. The dark blue waistcoat, which was no longer visible, now had a lower collar and coloured shoulder straps. The black or white gaiters no longer extended over the knee.

The 1812 dress regulations also introduced a new model of shako, with a new kind of brass frontal plate that bore a crowned Imperial Eagle atop a semi-circular plate into which the unit number was cut. The usual tricolour cockade and brass chinscales of the previous model of shako were retained. Cords and flounders were officially abolished, but in practice they continued to be worn by most of the regiments. The new shako had a red tufted pompom on the front (half-red and half-black for miners). The 1812 dress regulations introduced a new model of fatigue cap that replaced the previous bonnet de police; this was known as the pokalem and was a pie-shaped dark blue cap with a folding neck-flap that could be fastened under the chin. The pokalem was piped in red and bore a red badge consisting of two crossed axes on the front.

During the brief restoration of the Bourbons in 1814, some elements of the engineer uniform were modified: the tricolour cockade was replaced with the royal white one and a new shako plate bearing the coat-of-arms of the royal family came into use. The train of the Engineer Corps was dressed, like the Artillery Train, in iron-grey, but with black facings instead of dark blue ones.

Above left: Private of the engineers with M1812 uniform.

Above right: Private of the Train of the Equipment with M1812 dress.

Train of the Equipment Uniforms

In 1807 the uniform assigned to the Train of the Equipment was: black shako with brown pompom, half-red and half-brown plume, brown cords and flounders, tricolour national cockade with brown lace holder, white metal chinscale and white metal frontal plate bearing an Imperial Eagle above unit number; iron grey coat with brown collar and front lapels piped in iron-grey, brown pointed cuffs, brown turn-backs, iron-grey shoulder straps piped in brown, iron-grey five-pointed star badges on the turn-backs, white waistcoat, white breeches and black leather boots. On campaign, the breeches were replaced with iron-grey overalls incorporating side buttons and leather reinforcements, which were quite popular.

In 1812, the Train of the Equipment was given the new habit-veste and the new brass plate for the shako; as a result, its uniform was: black shako with tricolour national cockade, brown pompom, white metal chinscale and white metal frontal plate bearing an Imperial Eagle above a crescent with unit number; iron-grey habit-veste with brown collar, round cuffs, frontal plastron and short turn-backs, iron-grey cuff flaps and shoulder straps piped in brown, iron-grey five-pointed star badges on the turn-backs, white breeches or iron grey overalls, black leather boots.

Until 1812, the musicians of the Train of the Equipment were dressed in uniforms having reversed regimental colours. With the new dress regulations of that year, they were given the Imperial livery. Belt equipment was white and all ranks wore white leather gauntlet-like gloves. The saddlecoth consisted of a white half-shabraque made of sheepskin edged with small triangles of brown cloth, and of an iron grey shabraque edged in white.

Bibliography

Brnardic V, *Napoleon's Balkan Troops*, Osprey Publishing, 2004

Bucquoy E L, *Dragons et Guides d'Etat-Major*, Editions Grancher, 1977–85

Bucquoy E L, *Fanfares et Musiques*, Grancher, 1977–85

Bucquoy E L, *Gardes d'honneur et troupes étrangères*, Grancher, 1977–85

Bucquoy E L, *La Cavalerie légère*, Grancher, 1977–85

Bucquoy E L, *Le Passepoil*, Grancher, 1977–85

Bucquoy E L, *Les Cuirassiers*, Grancher, 1977–85

Bukhari E, *French Napoleonic Line Infantry 1796–1815*, Almark Publishing, 1973

Bukhari E, *Napoleon's Cuirassiers and Carabiniers*, Osprey Publishing, 1977

Bukhari E, *Napoleon's Dragoons and Lancers*, Osprey Publishing, 1976

Bukhari E, *Napoleon's Hussars*, Osprey Publishing, 1978

Bukhari E, *Napoleon's Line Chasseurs*, Osprey Publishing, 1977

Chartrand R, *Napoleon's Overseas Army*, Osprey Publishing, 1989

Chartrand R, *Napoleon's Sea Soldiers*, Osprey Publishing, 1990

Crowdy T, *French Napoleonic Infantryman 1803–1815*, Osprey Publishing, 2002

Crowdy T, *French Revolutionary Infantry 1789–1802*, Osprey Publishing, 2004

Crowdy T, *French Revolutionary Infantryman 1793–1815*, Osprey Publishing, 2003

Dempsey G C, *Napoleon's Mercenaries: Foreign Units in the French Army under the Consulate and Empire 1799 to 1814*, Frontline Books, 2016

Elting J R, *Napoleonic Uniforms*, Pearson, 1993–2000

Elting J R, *Swords Around a Throne: Napoleon's Grande Armée*, Free Press, 1988

Fieffé E, *Histoire des Troupes Etrangères au Service de France*, Librairie Militaire, 1854

Funcken F and Funcken L, *Les Soldats de la Revolution Française*, Casterman, 1988

Greentree D and Campbell D, *Napoleon's Swiss Troops*, Osprey Publishing, 2012

Haythornthwaite P, *Napoleon's Light Infantry*, Osprey Publishing, 1983

Haythornthwaite P, *Napoleon's Line Infantry*, Osprey Publishing, 1983

Haythornthwaite P, *Napoleon's Specialist Troops*, Osprey Publishing, 1988

Haythornthwaite P, *Uniforms of the Peninsular War 1807–1814*, Blandford Press, 1978

Haythornthwaite P, *Uniforms of the Retreat from Moscow 1812*, Blandford Press, 1976

Haythornthwaite P, *Uniforms of Waterloo*, Blandford Press, 1986

Jouineau A and Mongin J M, *French Line Infantry 1776–1810*, Editions Heimdal, 2021

Jouineau A and Mongin J M, *The Swiss at the service of France 1715–1820*, Editions Heimdal, 2019

Morawski R and Dusiewicz A, *The Polish Army Under Napoleon's Command*, Karabela Publishing, 2010

Pawly R, *Napoleon's Carabiniers*, Osprey Publishing, 2005

Wilkinson-Latham R, *Napoleon's Artillery*, Osprey Publishing, 1975

The Re-enactors

Association Jean Roch Coignet, Premier Bataillon du Premier Régiment de Grenadiers à Pied de la Garde Impériale

Jean Roch Coignet Association was founded in 1989 at Migennes (Bourgogne, France) by Pierre Pagès. Originally, the Association was active in making and painting historical figurines. Pierre Pagès began his First Empire historical re-enactment in 1990. It was natural for him to give to his association the name of Jean Roch Coignet, one of the most famous memoirists of the First Empire and also a Burgundian. For more than 20 years, the association has travelled in Europe to perpetuate the memory of the brave Napoleonic Army, being proud to wear the uniform of the First Battalion, First Regiment of Grenadiers of the Imperial Guard. From Madrid to Austerlitz, from Moscow to Leipzig, from Malta to Waterloo, the association allows everyone to re-live the Napoleonic era, presenting to the audience the uniforms and equipment of the Grenadiers of the Imperial Guard and the dress and materiel of the Great Army's women during bivouacs, military manoeuvres, parades and battles.

Contact
Website: http://www.associationjrcoignet.fr/
Email: associationjrcoignet@gmail.com
Facebook: https://www.facebook.com/associationjrcoignet

Le Livre, l'Histoire et l'Obusier

An historical re-enactment group whose main focus is the Imperial Guard's foot artillery (1804–15), but accepts members with all types of uniforms of the period. The group's speciality is the reconstruction of material of the time. It has two 4-pounder pieces, a 6-inch howitzer, two 5-inch 7-line mortars, a rolling kitchen, a removable field forge and a staff tent. The group is in the process of manufacturing a rolling bread oven. This set of equipment, unique in the world, is visible during its services in France or internationally. The association is located near Nancy, Lorraine, France.

Contact
Website: https://www.lelivrelhistoireetlobusier.fr/pages/index.html.html
Facebook: https://www.facebook.com/obusier/

2ème Régiment de Dragons

It was near the battlefield of Waterloo and its famous lion mount that a group of friends passionate about history and horse riding met in 1993 to form what would become one of the most important Napoleonic cavalry groups in central Europe. One of the founding members served in the 2nd Regiment of Dragoons, the oldest cavalry regiment in the French Army, which is still operational, thus the choice of the regiment the group would represent was obvious.

Riders quickly felt at ease during historical re-enactments. The group includes a dozen riders and grooms, some of whom have been horse professionals. 'Vivandières' take care of feeding hungry troops; the meals are cooked over a wood fire, just as they would have been.

Contact
Website: https://www.2dragons.be/

Les chasseurs à Cheval de la Grande Armée – 12ème Régiment

The association was created in 2007 and chose to approach re-enactment with ambitious requirements. It is composed of horse-riders eager to understand how, more than two centuries ago, soldiers and their mounts were able to cross Europe, fighting victoriously. The uniform retained by the association is characteristic of the chasseurs à cheval, and covers the most emblematic period of the Empire. The 12th Regiment was one of three regiments who accompanied the Emperor in his campaigns from 1805 to 1815. Rigour in uniformology, implementation of regulations and equestrian practice are among the aspects that this association has mastered.

Contact

Email: 12emechasseurs@hotmail.fr

Facebook: www.facebook.com/12emechasseurs/

33ème Regiment d'Infanterie de Ligne

Le 33ème Régiment d'Infanterie de Ligne is a group of enthusiasts operating in the Republic of Poland from 2013. It is the largest group in the country re-enacting French line infantry from the era of the Napoleonic Wars. The group members have uniforms according to different dates and army regulations, between 1796–1815. The group operates as part of the international project called Bataillon Uni. It takes part in events including the anniversaries of the following battles: Malta (1798), Austerlitz (1805), Jena (1806), Gołymin (1806), Heilsberg (1807), Jonkowo-Barkweda (1807), Kłodzko (1807), Grudziądz (1807), Znojmo (1809), Daugavpils (1812), Leipzig (1813) and Waterloo (1815). The group is to reconstructs the realities and uniforms of the era, the customs of soldiers, their everyday life, great battles and the hardships of the campaigns.

Contact

Email: 33emeregiment@gmail.com

Facebook: www.facebook.com/33deligne/

Pascal Thonon is a self-taught photographer and an artist at heart. He has carefully captured the artistry of the re-enactors for this title.

Contact

Website: https://thononphotography.wixsite.com/monsite

Voltigeurs of the 18th Line Regiment

The Voltigeurs of the 18th Line Regiment live the history and reconstruct the lives of Napoleonic soldiers, travelling all over Europe. Together its members study history, live it and educate the public. The group is a member of La Charte d'Histoire Vivante, the Napoleonic Military Living-Historian Charter. Members come from Central Europe and the group is based in the Czech Republic.

Contact

Email: 18e.voltigeurs@gmail.com

Facebook: www.facebook.com/voltigeurs18e

Other books you might like:

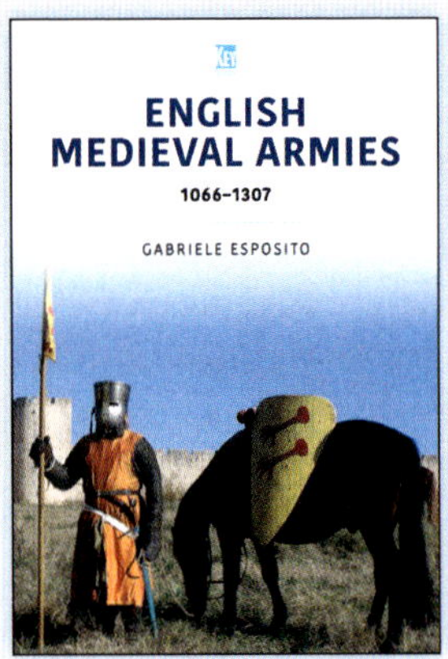

Historic Armies Series,
Vol. 1

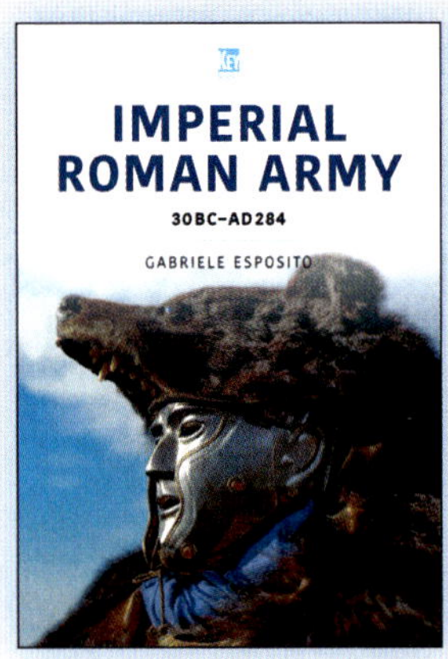

Historic Armies Series,
Vol. 2

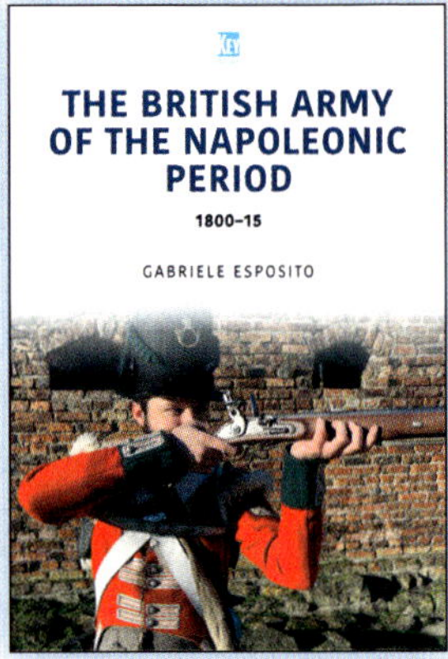

Historic Armies Series,
Vol. 3

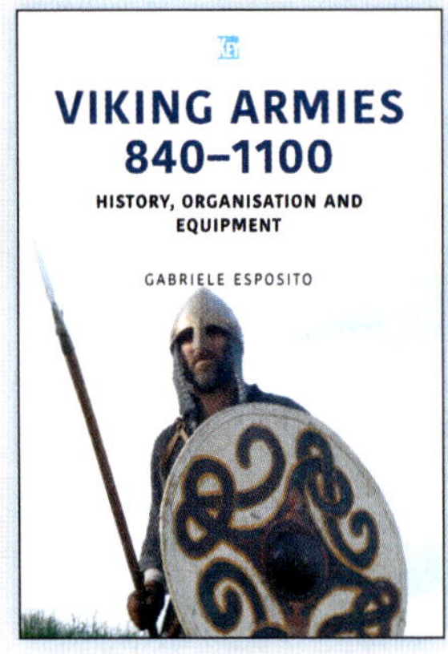

Historic Armies Series,
Vol. 4

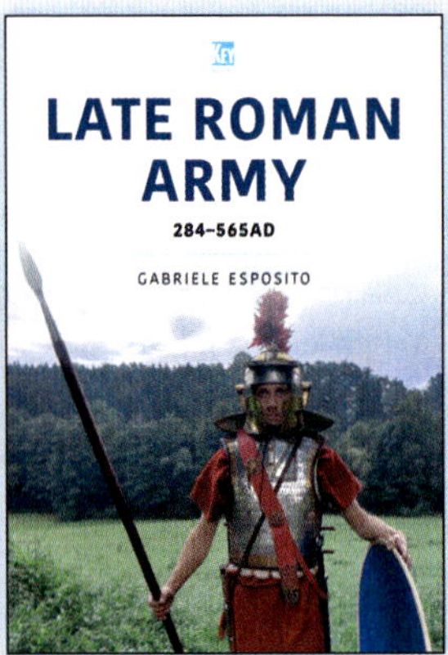

Historic Armies Series,
Vol. 5

For our full range of titles please visit:
shop.keypublishing.com/books

VIP Book Club

Sign up today and receive
TWO FREE E-BOOKS

Be the first to find out about our forthcoming
book releases and receive exclusive offers.

Register now at **keypublishing.com/vip-book-club**

*Our VIP Book Club is a 100% spam-free zone, and we will never share your email with anyone else.
You can read our full privacy policy at: privacy.keypublishing.com*